Crete

Front cover: Préveli Monastery

Below: a Minoan fresco at Knossos

TOP 10 ATTRACTIONS

Archaeological Museum of Iráklio Packed with priceless Minoan finds *(page 36)*

Ágios Nikólaos The prettiest town in the east of the island is a popular resort that preserves its Cretan charm *(page 55)*

Samariá Gorge The longest gorge in Europe is a strenuous but exhilarating trek *(page 84)*

Moní Arkadíou A shrine to the Cretan struggle for independence *(page 74)*

Haniá The minaret-style lighthouse and scenic harbour are amongst many of Haniá's highlights *(page 79)*

Moní Toploú A peaceful place with a bloody history *(page 65)*

Gortys The capital of Crete in Roman and Byzantine times *(page 46)*

Knossos Its Minoan palace, with superb frescoes, is Crete's most visited attraction *(page 41)*

Lasíthi Plateau Home to rural life and ancient windmills *(page 61)*

Réthymno Réthymno's attractive Venetian harbour is lined with dozens of fish restaurants *(page 71)*

A PERFECT TOUR

Pick up your hire car at Iráklio airport, check into a city hotel and look round the Archaeological Museum. Stroll through the old quarter, taking in the Historical and Religious Art museums (see pages 34 and 36) in particular. Devote the following morning to Knossos Palace.

Day 5 Swim and overnight in Mýrtos

Proceed via Zíros and Makrý Gialós, stopping to swim at a tempting beach, before a lunch (and museum) stop in Ierápetra. Continue west to overnight at peaceful Mýrtos.

Days 3–4 Head east

Lunch in Ágios Nikólaos, then head east via Sitía to Moní Toploú and Vaï beach. Stay over near Koureménos beach for two nights. On day 4, hike the Hohlahiés gorge, and sample windsurfing at Koureménos.

Days 6–7 Rouvás Gorge

Drive inland from Mýrtos towards the Mesará valley, pausing at Áno Viánnos for its brilliantly frescoed church, before proceeding to Zarós for two overnights. On day 7, walk the Rouvás Gorge or visit the monastic churches of Vrondísi and Ágios Fanoúrios. With any time remaining, make the short detour to ancient Gortys.

Days 2–3 Ágios Nikólaos and Spinalónga Island

After lunch in Iráklio, drive east to Ágios Nikólaos, choosing accommodation nearby. Take in 'Ag Nik's' lakeside nightlife, then next morning embark at Pláka for Spinalónga Island to visit its abandoned leper colony.

OF CRETE

Days 10–11 Sightseeing in Réthymno

Drive to Réthymno, stopping at Arkádi monastery en route, and arrange lodging in the atmospheric old town for two nights. Spend the entire next day taking in the old quarter, especially the massive Fortezza and the Historical and Folklore Museum.

Days 14–15 Hike

Park your hire car safely before taking a dawn bus up to Xylóskala for the unmissable descent of the Samariá Gorge. At the bottom, overnight at Agía Rouméli; next day, take a boat west to Soúgia or Paleóhora where you will have an opportunity for another well-deserved swim. Finally, take a bus back to Haniá, retrieve your car, and drive to your departure airport.

Day 8–9 Church visit

Continue west, via the Minoan highlights of Phaistos and Agía Triáda, pausing for lunch at either Vóri or Mátala (swim at the latter). End the day at Plakiás or Spíli, checking in for two nights. The next day involves an early start to tour the Amári Valley to visit its churches, with possibly time late in the afternoon for a swim at Ágios Pávlos beach.

Days 12–13 West towards Haniá

Proceed west towards Haniá, stopping for a swim and lunch at idyllic Lake Kourná. Arrive in Haniá for a two-night stay at a boutique hotel in the old quarter. The afternoon and the whole of day 13 are spent savouring the old town's museums, shops and plentiful restaurants.

CONTENTS

30

70

11

97

108

54

Features

INTRODUCTION

Crete: the name invokes a range of different images. Ancient sites to explore; commercial towns bustling with noise and traffic; millions of olive trees blanketing the countryside; raucous resorts with neon-lit bars and loud music; a romantic meal for two overlooking a small fishing port; mountains and gorges to trek through; a sun-bed on a beach among hundreds of others similarly soaking up the rays; 15 hours of sunshine a day in summer; three feet of snow in the mountains in winter. This island has something for everyone, and its sheer variety satisfies even the most jaded and cynical traveller.

The 'Great Island'

Crete sits in the eastern Mediterranean Sea, just 110 nautical miles north of the African coast and an even shorter sea-crossing from Anatolia. Its strategic position at the crossroads of trade north from Egypt, west from Rome and east from the Middle East, made it valuable territory from the earliest days of trade and power politics.

With an area of 8,300 sq km (3,200 sq miles), Crete is sometimes called Megalónissos, or 'Great Island'. Visually it is stunning, with three dramatic mountain ranges over 2,000m (6,500ft) high that seem to anchor the island in the sea. Water has cut vertiginous gorges through the mountains and opened huge cave systems through their

The beautiful lagoon at Elafónisos, west of Haniá

Crete's provinces

Crete is divided into four administrative districts (*periféries* in Greek), mostly named after their governing cities: Iráklio, the most populous, with the island's capital; Haniá; Lasíthi (based in Ágios Nikólaos); and Réthymno.

hearts. These caves were places of great religious significance to the ancient Cretans; in some cases they were thought to be the birthplaces of Greek gods. Over the centuries these caverns provided protection for pirates, vagabonds and freedom fighters. The mountains were never fully conquered, even during World War II – their furthest valleys were too remote, their slopes too steep. Today, their peaks are the domain of numerous birds of prey, including eagles, hawks and vultures.

Fertile plateaus and lowlands have been settled and farmed since Neolithic times; abundant fresh spring water from the surrounding peaks helped ensure a rich harvest. Around the coastline – especially in the north – long sandy stretches have attracted visitors since the 1960s advent of package tours, but variety exists here too, with several different coastal environments – rocky coves, rugged headlands and marshy wetlands.

The Fruitful Year

Despite its southerly latitude, seasons remain distinct on Crete. Springtime sees the hills awash with flowers and wheat crops ripening in the warming sun, goat kids are born and the flocks make the most of fresh pastures. As summer starts, the cereals are harvested and the land takes on an ochre hue. Birdsong gives way to the sound of cicada, and the smell of honeysuckle rises in the evening air. Midsummer sees Cretans seeking shade to escape the heat, while visitors head out in droves to work on their tans. The clanging of livestock bells can be heard across the countryside as flocks desper-

Natural landscape

ately search for sustenance in the parched hills.

Autumn brings a cooling of the temperature yet a warming of the landscape, as colours mellow in the lower arc of the late season sun. Stucco on buildings takes on a rosy hue, the grapes swell to tempting perfection, and citrus fruit begin their transition from green to orange. Soon, winter brings a blanket of snow to the mountains; ordinarily dry ravines and pastures swell with rain run off; wood smoke fills the air, and the old folks retreat to their warm hearths.

The olive harvest is the main focal point of the year. This crop reigns supreme and millions of trees blanket hillside slopes and coastal plains, a symbol of man's reliance on the earth. It has sustained Cretans for too long to be treated with disdain.

Sheep are raised both for milk and meat

The Cradle of Europe

The footsteps of history can be seen on every dusty path and urban street. Crete was the cradle of European civilisation, and the Minoans – a people believed to be mythological until evidence of their existence was confirmed early in the 20th century – travelled far and wide across the eastern Mediterranean for trade.

A prodigious collection of artefacts now displayed in museums across the island shows them to be the first indigenous European culture, whose lives were graced by art, sports and the pursuit of pleasure. The Minoan civilisation suffered a sudden and terminal collapse around 1450BC for reasons that have not been fully established.

A devastating natural disaster was initially thought to be the cause, but archaeological theories now consider either invasion by a warring people or internal revolt to be the most likely scenarios. Whatever the case, the catastrophe heralded the start of thousands of years of invasion and subjection for the Cretans. Mycenaeans, Dorians, Athenians, Macedonians, Romans, Byzantines, Arabs, Venetians and Ottomans all came to take control. Evidence of their presence abounds in the commanding fortresses, protective harbours, fine mansions, narrow winding alleys, elegant minarets and ornate fountains of the towns. In 1913 Crete finally achieved a long awaited *énosis* (union) with Orthodox Christian Greece.

Freedom or Death

Cretans did not take kindly to their native land being usurped and, particularly in the years of Turkish rule, they gained a reputation as formidable and tenacious fighters who would strike with speed and then retreat to mountain strongholds to outwit their enemies.

The remains of Crete's first monastery, Katholikó

They reverted back to the same lifestyle during World War II when Crete was captured by German forces, mounting a successful guerrilla resistance and living up to the old rallying cry – 'freedom or death'.

Invaders would occupy the cities but they could never manage to tame the people of the countryside. For centuries, unbowed Cretans lived simple lives in harmony with the land, tending their flocks, growing fruit and vegetables, and harvesting the sea.

Clothes and carpets were made of wool, leather was used to make boots and saddles, wood was used for bowls and utensils, and grass and straw woven into basketry. Seasonal surpluses were stored to provide sustenance for the long winters that often isolated mountain

El Greco was born in Fódele

villages. The people put their trust in God, as the many Orthodox churches across the island attest, praying for self-determination and for their menfolk hiding out in the hills.

Enduring Traditions

Although peace now reigns, a glance around communities in the Cretan heartland still suggests that little has changed. White-washed villages dot the landscape, each house with its own smallholding. The traditional diet – greens, olive oil, wild herbs, honey, yoghurt and a little lamb or goat meat – still sustains these rural people, and it has been scientifically proven to be one of the healthiest in the world. And, though the traditions are dying, some older men still stride out in the black breeches, leather boots and crocheted headbands worn by previous generations; widows in black sit quietly knitting in their doorways; and goats graze slopes that no farmer could use.

If a Cretan's hatred of his enemy is legendary, it has always been surpassed by generosity to his friends – and by extension to strangers (*xénos* is the Greek word for both stranger and friend). A door is always open to a passing traveller. Today, admiring an orchard or a ripening vineyard even in rudimentary Greek will result in an armful of fruit to take with you on your journey – just a small example of how tradition carries on through the generations. And how do today's Cretans find their pleasure? Poetry, literature, music and dance; traditional forms of all these arts are still alive and well here.

Yet despite its traditions, Crete is also a very modern, and urbanised, island; since the 1980s many remote interior villages have all but emptied in favour of the largest coastal towns, which are expanding constantly. Young Cretans are

Conflict of Interests

Prosperity alters much that it touches. The difference in living standards, between those people directly benefiting from the tourist trade and those who are not involved, has in some cases led to social divisions. This happens not just around the coastal resorts, but inland, particularly as the newly enriched return to build opulent mansions in dilapidated ancestral villages.

But it would be a mistake to see only the negative side of tourism on Crete. The island has no natural resources in terms of minerals or petroleum, and, apart from the huge agricultural economy and some windfarms, little other enterprise. Seasonal tourism is often the only relief from winter unemployment that top 20 percent in some spots. One must hope that development is kept within reasonable limits, so that tourism will remain a blessing for visitors and islanders alike.

just as interested in fashion, higher education and music as their peninsular-Greek cousins. They aim to find jobs with excitement, a secure future and ready cash to spend – something they feel a rural way of life cannot give them. Even in the present economic downturn, the three largest north-coast towns of Iráklio, Réthymno and Haniá have active commercial sectors and vibrant intellectual scenes thanks to their universities and polytechnics, aspects of Crete that surprise many visitors.

Mass tourism has changed the face of the north coast

Of course the arrival of mass tourism has changed Crete, particularly along the northern coast where the majority of the development has taken place. The island is invaded annually by an army of tourists who flock here searching for sunshine, relaxation and fun, and Cretans seem happy to welcome everyone with precisely the kinds of activities that holidaymakers demand. However, there's just too much land area and too much individuality here for Crete ever to become just another 'Euro-island'. Fears of a cultural meltdown, while perhaps understandable, are wide of the mark. Gritty and enduring as ever, Cretans will continue to do things their way. This cultural distinction, its fascinating history and the dramatic landscape will make Crete an enthralling holiday destination for decades to come.

A BRIEF HISTORY

Crete's long history is bound up with its strategic position between Western Europe, the Middle East and North Africa. In good times this brought trade, ideas and prosperity; in bad times, invasion, oppression and disease. Many fascinating legacies around the island attest to the complicated web that time has spun here.

The earliest human remains found on Crete date back to the seventh millennium BC. These first inhabitants were Neolithic hunter-gatherers who came from Asia Minor. They developed into farmers, with settlements and pastureland on the fertile Messará Plain. It was an influx of new, more skilled settlers shortly after 3000BC that ushered in the Minoan era, the first major civilisation to arise on European soil.

The Minoans

A great ancient Cretan civilisation was for many years believed to be merely the stuff of mythology. Yet with the discovery of cities and their marvellous artefacts, Sir Arthur Evans, its principal advocate, made reality out of folklore and myth *(see page 41)*. We now know many facts about Minoan Crete – including that, at its zenith, the population of the island probably numbered more than two million, approximately four times greater than today's figure, with 100,000 people living in the capital, Knossos.

These early Bronze Age settlements were built without fortifications and comprised vast numbers of

Bronze-Age Crete

Arthur Evans classified the three periods of Bronze-Age Crete as Early, Middle and Late Minoan, minutely subdivided. They are now known as the Pre-Palatial, Proto-Palatial, Neo-Palatial and Post-Palatial eras.

A 3,500-year-old fresco of three Minoan women in Knossos

dwellings. The cities developed organically rather than to any grand design. The first palatial structures at Knossos, and other great cities such as Phaestos (modern Festós) and Malia, were erected between 2000–1900BC, but these were all destroyed by an earthquake around 1700BC. The remains visible today are their replacements, even bigger and more splendid than the originals. This golden age of Minoan society – known as the Neo-Palatial era – lasted about 250 years.

The Minoans were ruled by a priest-king who presided over both religious and economic affairs. It is unclear whether he reigned over the entire island, or if each palace settlement had its own regional king. His people worshipped the Mother Goddess, and divine power was symbolised by the bull, the focus of ornate and elaborate rituals. One sacred symbol, at odds with their peaceful lifestyle, is the *labrys* (double-headed axe). Its image has been found on various artefacts throughout the island.

Exquisite gold jewellery from
Mália, probably a burial offering

The Minoans developed an alphabet and printing method, along with sophisticated plumbing and water-delivery systems. Women enjoyed high status, playing an active part in palace life, and the whole population enjoyed athletic contests, games and a whole range of recreational activities. Above all, they excelled in the visual arts.

Wherever there was a blank 'canvas' there was imagery: decorative entrances, walls, floors and pottery. Many breathtaking examples can be seen in the Archaeological Museum in Iráklio (see page 36). Even the smallest items, such as combs, were exquisitely worked. Gold and precious stones were fashioned into beautiful jewellery, which indicates a high quality of life for at least certain classes of people.

What fuelled this great empire was trade. Cretans exhibited their skills not only with local resources such as paint, clay, copper and bronze, but also with imported raw materials – lapis lazuli from Afghanistan, ivory from Syria, gold, silver and black obsidian from Anatolia. Copper and bronze were worked and re-exported, along with high-value foodstuffs such as olive oil, honey and wine.

The Minoans developed into one of the great naval powers of the Mediterranean, with wood from the island's vast juniper and cypress forests providing material for boats. However, they concentrated their power more on commercial than military gain, showing a taste for the good life rather than a hunger for an empire.

This great civilisation came to a sudden, catastrophic end in around 1450BC. The exact cause remains unknown, but all the palaces were destroyed at the same time. Charred remains at Knossos and ash at Zakros suggest a great conflagration. A leading theory for many years was that natural disaster struck the island in the wake of the volcanic explosion on the island of Thíra (Santoríni), due north of Crete, bringing tidal waves, earthquakes and fire storms. But Thíra exploded in about 1500BC, a half-century before the Cretan destruction; more recent research has favoured another hypothesis – that an attack by invaders or domestic rebel forces may have brought about the end of this fine culture. Scholars will continue to debate the reason for many years to come.

Lató was the dominant city during the Dorian occupation

Dorians and Romans

After the disaster, Mycenaean Greeks from the Peloponnese moved in to control what remained of the Minoan settlements – they may even have precipitated the destruction. Around 1200BC, Dorian invaders from the Balkans drove south through the Greek mainland, across the Aegean and into Crete.

Many coastal dwellers migrated to remote mountain settlements in order to escape their enemies. Others embarked on an overseas

The complex legal code of Gortys was carved in stone

exodus that took them around the Mediterranean Sea. The island did not get directly involved in Greece's Persian and Peloponnesian Wars, although it became a valuable source of brave and energetic mercenaries.

While mainland Greece was reaching its zenith during the Classical Age (480–338BC), Crete remained a backwater of warring city-states, of which Gortys (modern Górtyna) was the most powerful. Nevertheless, enlightened Athenians acknowledged Crete as a source of much of their culture, and its caves and shrines were major centres of pilgrimage. The island's most important achievement – and only significant remnant – from this period is the law code of Gortys *(see page 46)*. It reveals a hierarchical society of free men, serfs and slaves ruled by an aristocratic class.

It took the Romans three years of brutal fighting to conquer Crete in 67BC, and they did so only by playing the rival city-states against one another. Crete remained a province of the Roman Empire until AD395, with Gortys as its capital. The Romans brought a certain order to the island, putting an end to internal struggles, building new roads, ports and aqueducts, and introducing systems of domestic plumbing and central heating not much worse than those found today.

Early Christians

The apostle Paul arrived in AD60–61, and by AD64 had charged his disciple Titus to convert the islanders to Christianity. Titus had a hard time combating local pagan beliefs, but died peacefully in AD107, as bishop of Gortys, and Titus (Ágios Títos in Greek) became Crete's patron saint.

When Roman power split in two, the eastern Byzantine Empire inherited the island (though its hold on islands in the south Aegean were, in reality, nominal). Attacks by pirates and Islamic forces brought terror to the people, but Cretans remained loyal to the Orthodox Church throughout the occupation, by Andalucian pirates, of AD824–961. The island was recaptured after a terrible siege of Iráklio by Byzantine commander (and subsequently emperor) Nikeforos Phokas, during which he catapulted the heads of dead Arabs into the city to dishearten surviving defenders.

Venetian Days

After Byzantium fell to the Crusaders in 1204, Crete was given to their leader, Boniface of Montferrat, who immediately sold it to Venice for 1,000 silver marks, ushering in a new era. Crete

The Church's role

The Greek Orthodox Church has always played a special role on Crete. Under foreign domination, the Church funded and organised schools where Greek language and traditions were taught and kept alive. Most significantly, it was the focus of unity and resistance to oppression, as indicated by the many attacks on Crete's 34 monasteries.

Byzantine-style icon painting flourished under the Venetians

prospered greatly under the 465 years of Venetian occupation (1204–1669), although during the first century there were repeated revolts by both Venetian colonists and displaced Byzantine aristocracy. As a source of shipbuilding timber in a key location, the island was a linchpin in the far-flung commercial empire, and became the Republic's first formally constituted overseas colony.

Proudly emblazoned with the Lion of St Mark, the ports and fortifications of Iráklio (called Candia under Venetian rule, as was the whole of Crete), Haniá and Réthymno bear witness to the Venetians' ambitious public building programme. Several handsome villas and loggias still attest to their gracious style of living. After the 14th century, native upper-class Cretans began to intermarry with the occupiers and to participate in their style of government.

The arts flourished during the 15th and 16th centuries, a period known as the Cretan Renaissance. Numerous new monasteries and churches were built. Icon-painting attained new heights after an influx of artists from around Byzantium after 1453, who founded important schools of art.

The great literary figure of the time, Vitsentzos Kornaros (1553–1613), wrote a romantic epic poem in Cretan dialect, the *Erotokritos*. Even if most villagers can no longer recite it by heart, it is still acclaimed among the literati of Crete.

The Battle for Crete

In the eastern Mediterranean, Christian forces were in retreat as a new Muslim power began to expand. The Ottoman Turks pushed Venetian and Genoese forces out of Asia Minor and the Greek mainland, and then from most islands of the Aegean. Eventually it would be Crete's turn. The Ottomans waged a titanic war to wrest the island from the Venetians. It began with raids on Haniá, Réthymno and Sitía in the 1530s by the notorious pirate-admiral Hayreddin Barbarossa. Over the next century, the Venetians greatly strengthened the fortifications, but Haniá and Réthymno fell anyway in 1645.

Two years later, the Turks laid siege to the capital, Candia.

The Cretan Renaissance

After the fall of Constantinople in 1453, Crete became a haven for artists and theologians fleeing the Ottomans. A religious college for the study of painting, theology and the humanities was established at the Church of Agía Ekateríni in Iráklio (*see page 36*), which became the centre of the Cretan Renaissance during the 16th and 17th centuries. El Greco is said to have studied here, along with his contemporary Mihaïl Damaskinos, and Vitsentzos Kornaros, the author of the epic poem *Erotokritos*.

Cretan artists excelled at icon painting, blending traditional Byzantine style with influences from Renaissance Italy. Their work was in demand throughout the Western world. Damaskinos, who worked in Venice from 1577 to 1582, was the master of this art. His use of colour and perspective brought a depth to the icon tradition that was widely imitated.

It was an epic struggle, which was to last 22 years. Initially weakened by an outbreak of plague, the 12,000-strong population rallied to the defence. After 15 years, the Turkish commander, Hüseyin Pasha, was summoned back to Constantinople and publicly strangled for his failure to take the city. Supposedly 30,000 defenders died, but there were 118,000 fatalities among the besiegers.

Although Western Europe's leaders watched with bated breath, they sent little support, and inexorably Venetian resistance was worn down. As the conquerors entered the city gates in 1699, the Venetians negotiated an orderly departure, taking with them, among other Christian artefacts, the head of St Titus. This most cherished of Crete's religious relics was not to return to the island until 1966.

Ottoman Rule

Crete's years spent under the Ottomans (1669–1898) largely constituted a period of cultural and economic stagnation. Imperial leaders had no interest in developing or investing in this new domain and, after the occasionally oppressive but often brilliant centuries of Venetian government, Crete slid back into a dark age.

Apart from repairing the islands' fortifications, the Ottomans left relatively few lasting remnants of their rule. They built few mosques – largely because many Cretan converts adhered to the heterodox Bektaşi sect – and left only a few houses in the largest towns, where they made up nearly half of the population until the 1840s. Most numerous of their legacies are the ornate street

> **National day**
>
> Crete celebrates its National Day on 8 November, the anniversary of the explosion in 1866 at Arkádi Monastery, where hundreds of Cretan rebels died rather than surrender to the Turks.

Monastery of martyrs: Arkádi is a shrine to Cretan resistance

fountains found in the corners of market squares and outside chapels. Throughout this period, many town-dwelling Cretans kept a low profile. They publicly converted to Islam to escape heavy taxes, continuing to practise their Orthodox faith in secret.

There were sporadic attempts at revolt, which were often launched from remote mountain strongholds where rebels could survive in safety. The more vulnerable communities on the lower plains paid a high price for these revolts in the form of swift bloody reprisals.

The first major rebellion occurred in 1770 when the Russians, hoping to distract the Turks while they waged their own attacks on the Ottoman Empire elsewhere, promised aid to Daskalogiannis, a wealthy shipowner. He raised a revolt in Sfakiá, but the support never arrived. The rebellion was crushed, Daskalogiannis was flayed alive, and the event became the subject of a rousing epic poem.

However, once part of Greece had achieved independence from the Ottoman Empire after 1830, the atmosphere changed. After two decades of rule by an Egyptian vassal of the sultan, various forms of semi-autonomous rule, with representation for Christian notables, were attempted, but to no avail. Insurgencies recurred, generally put down with considerable severity; for the Cretan resisters death came to form a monumental collective badge of honour.

During the major 1866 uprising, hundreds of Christian Cretans – and many Muslims – died in a suicide explosion at Arkádi Monastery. There were more insurgencies in 1889 and 1895. The island's repeated suffering was duly celebrated in the popular, heroic *Songs of Digenis* (adapted from their medieval origins for the modern struggle), Pandelis Prevelakis' particularly grim novel *The Cretan*, and the lofty writings of Níkos Kazantzákis.

Union with Greece

Finally, in 1898, the European powers forced the Ottomans to grant Crete autonomy within the empire and accept Prince

Cretan Eleftherios Venizelos brought union with Greece

George, second son of King George of Greece, as high commissioner. This did not satisfy Cretan nationalists, and the prince, presiding over an island divided into ultra-nationalist and accommodationist parliamentary factions, resigned in 1906. It was only in 1913, under the leadership of the Cretan Eleftherios Venizelos, that *énosis* (union) with Greece was achieved.

Despite being unscathed by World War I, Crete saw major changes between 1913 and the mid-1920s. Muslim Cretans had been leaving for Rhodes, the Middle East and Anatolia since 1897, but the disastrous 1919–22 Greek invasion of Turkey, and the ultimately successful Turkish resistance to it, greatly accelerated this movement through the compulsory population exchange between Greece and Turkey in 1923. The last of thousands of Muslims were expelled, with Orthodox refugees from Asia Minor arriving to take their place.

The dead of two world wars lie in Haniá's British War Cemetery

War and Peace

Yet Crete's travails were not yet over. During World War II, the rapid advance of the German forces through mainland Greece in 1941 forced the Allies to retreat to Crete. On 20 May, German paratroops secured the airfield at Máleme, just west of Haniá. British, Australian and New Zealand soldiers joined Cretan militia during a valiant defence in the ten-day Battle of Crete, but were ultimately forced to retreat across the island. Many were evacuated to Egypt, though several thousand were left stranded and fled to the mountains. Casualties on both sides were terrible: Allied losses numbered 2,000 killed and 12,000 taken prisoner, while the German war cemetery contains almost 4,500 graves.

With their tradition of opposition to foreign invaders, Cretans immediately began resistance activities against the occupying German force. Initial efforts to shelter stranded Allied servicement and smuggle them off the island in small groups from isolated south-coast beaches were remarkably successful. But after the Italian capitulation in September 1943, brutal German reprisals against civilians became more frequent. In early 1944 the resistance pulled off an amazing coup by kidnapping the German commander, General Kreipe, and smuggling him off the island. Subsequently, German forces burnt many villages and killed many men of fighting age in the Amári Valley. The occupation of Crete did not completely end until May 1945, when the Germans abandoned Haniá. Many Cretan towns were left in ruins from heavy bombing, but Crete largely escaped the internal strife of the civil war that raged in mainland Greece (1946–49) and felt fewer effects of the oppressive colonels' junta (1967–74) than other Greek communities.

In 1981, Greece became a full member of the European Community, and Andreas Papandreou's PASOK party, with overwhelming support from Crete (who saw it as heir to the

Andreas Papandreou

Venizelist tradition), won elections to form Greece's first quasi-socialist government. Papandreou's son, George, became prime minister late in 2009, presiding over economic collapse and charged by Greece's creditors with essentially undoing most of his father's legacy, before being replaced by a technocratic unity coalition in November 2011.

Historical Landmarks

c. 6500–2600BC Settlers arrive in Crete from Asia Minor.

2600–2000BC Pre-Palatial era: immigrants bring copper and pottery.

2000–1700BC Proto-Palatial period: discovery of bronze; language written down; first palaces built, then destroyed by earthquake.

1700–1450BC Neo-Palatial era: the golden age of Minoan civilisation.

c.1450BC Minoan palaces destroyed; Mycenaeans arrive.

c.1150BC Dorians from northern Greece conquer most of Crete.

11th–1st centuries BC Crete consists of warring city states.

67BC Crete becomes a Roman province, with Gortys the capital.

c. AD 60–107 St Titus first bishop of Crete.

395 Roman Empire splits permanently, Crete allotted to Byzantium (Constantinople).

824–961 Arabs conquer Crete, destroy Gortys, make their capital at fortress of Rabdh el-Khandak (Iráklio).

961 Nikephoros Fokas recaptures Crete for Byzantium.

1204 Venetians acquire Crete, rule for 465 years from Candia (Iráklio).

15th–17th centuries Crete becomes the centre of Byzantine art.

1669 Turks capture Candia after 22-year seige and control all Crete.

1821–7 Greek War of Independence; Crete under Egyptian control.

1898 European Great Powers occupy Crete, which becomes an autonomous principality within the Ottoman Empire.

1913 Crete finally becomes part of Greece.

1923 Last Muslims expelled from Crete; Christians arrive from Asia Minor.

1941–5 Germany occupies Crete: heavy losses, villages destroyed.

Late 1960s Tourist boom begins.

1971 Iráklio replaces Haniá as capital of Crete.

1981 Greece joins the European Union. First socialist government.

2002 The euro becomes the currency of Greece.

2004 Greece hosts the Olympics in Athens.

2009 George Papandreou leads PASOK back to power.

2010–11 Greece effectively bankrupt, dependent on IMF/EU loans.

WHERE TO GO

Crete is a large island, so if you want to see a lot of what it has to offer, choose your itinerary carefully. Staying at a central base allows for excursions to both the east and west, whereas a base in the far east or west limits your ability to see the opposite end of the island.

This guide divides Crete into four sections: first the capital, Iráklio, followed by the central section; then we move east, before finally exploring the western parts of the island. The major attractions are covered, so that you can plan your itinerary around them, but remember that the countryside is filled with hidden treasures; traditional communities, frescoed churches and mountain paths. All of these are waiting to be discovered.

IRÁKLIO

Iráklio comes as a surprise to travellers used to Greek island ports further north in the Aegean Sea. It is the fourth-largest Greek city (population approximately 160,000), and the commercial and administrative heart of Crete. Despite current hard times – winter unemployment exceeds 20 percent – there is a lively scene based around the university, and a sophistication to match other medium-sized Greek university towns like Pátra or Ioánnina. However, this is not the only facet of the city. Around the harbour you'll still find a fishing industry based on small family-owned boats, and in the narrow backstreets a few surviving small workshops.

Truth be told, Iráklio is far from the most attractive town; heavy bombing during World War II was compounded by thoughtless postwar development, and only recently have its

The sizeable harbour at Iráklio

crumbling medieval quarters, public monuments and surviving older buildings gotten the preservation attention they deserve. But take time to explore the narrow lanes beyond the traffic-clogged main boulevards and you will be rewarded.

Iráklio was a thriving port in Minoan times and became known as Heracleum under Roman rule. The Andalusians who established the Emirate of Crete built a huge castle here, while the Venetians chose it as their capital, giving the name Candia to both the city and the whole island. Candia prospered from Venetian trade, and when Turkish forces stormed the island, the town held out for 22 years before falling in 1669. As Kandiye, it became a relative backwater of the Ottoman Empire, only to rise to prominence again following union with Greece. It was declared capital again in 1971, taking the title from Haniá in the west.

The City Centre

The city centre lies within the vast fortress started by the Venetians and reinforced by the Ottomans. One can walk along sections of its walls to gain an impression of how large the citadel once was. The heart of Iráklio is the small **Platía Venizélou** (Venizelos Square), with its fringe of cafés and restaurants. At its centre, the **Morosini Fountain** dates from Venetian times, though its sombre lion statues are 300 years older and lend the widely used nickname of Platía Leondária (Lions' Square). From here, most of Iráklio's attractions are only a few minutes' walk – the closest, flanking the plaza, being **Ágios Márkos** (St Mark's), a Venetian church now the municipal art gallery.

North along pedestrianised Ikostipémptis Avgoústou (25th August Street) looms the impressive façade of the **Venetian Loggia**, originally dating from 1628 but reconstructed after World War II. Iráklio's municipal offices divide themselves between here and the adjacent Andrógeio Mégaro. Walk around the loggia to find the **Church of Ágios Títos**. Founded late in

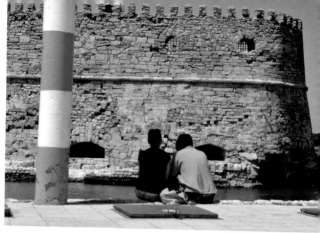

The Venetian fortress guards the harbour at Iráklio

the first millennium, it honours St Titus, the island's first bishop and patron saint. When the church was consecrated, Titus's body was brought here from Gortys and re-interred. The Venetians took his remains to Venice when they fled the island, and the church was rebuilt as the Vezir Mosque after an 1856 earthquake, resulting in the incongruous but beautiful decoration on the outer walls. In 1966 the Venetian authorities returned the skull of St Titus to Ágios Títos in a gold reliquary, along with fine paintings depicting scenes of the saint's life. Just west lies a small park supplied with more cafés – **El Greco** – named after the painter, a native of Crete, whose real name was Doménikos Theotokópoulos.

The Harbour Area

Continuing down 25th August Street leads to the waterfront and the majestic **Venetian fortress** (Koulés; Tue–Sun 8.30am–3pm) out on the breakwater, built to protect the old harbour. En route you'll pass vaulted remains of the large, arcaded *arsenália* (repair depots) that serviced Venetian ships, as well as the city's fishing fleet, small colourful boats with piles of yellow nets. The fortress was completed in 1540 to protect the town against the Ottoman threat, and, with the circuit of walls inland, explains how Candia held out long after the rest of Crete had fallen. A tour of the interior reveals a strong and efficient design; there are wonderful views from its ramparts.

A short walk west along the waterfront, past the disused Dominican monastery of Ágios Pétros (St Peter), brings you to the **Historical Museum of Crete** (Mon–Sat 9am–5pm; www.historical-museum.gr), housed in an impressive building that is part Venetian mansion, part modern glass edifice. The museum thematically rather than chronologically covers Cretan history from the Byzantine Empire to the present, as well as ethnography. There are exquisite icons and fresco fragments rescued from churches across the island, stone relief carvings, documentation of the local Jewish, Muslim and Armenian communities, folk textiles and a re-creation of a traditional Cretan home. Models and prints of Iráklio across the centuries show how the townscape has developed, as does an interactive model of the medieval city, showing the many monuments sadly destroyed since 1897. Due prominence is given to the struggle for Cretan independence and World War II resistance (including the 1942 sabotage of the local Ger-

What's in a name?

Iráklio was first named Heracleum by the Romans, before the Andalucian Arabs changed its name to Rabdh-al-Khandaq – becoming Hándax for the Greeks under Nikephoros Phokas who soon re-conquered it. The Venetians renamed it Candia. During the Ottoman occupation, Muslims knew it as Kandiye, while the Cretans called it Megalo Kastro (Big Fortress), until the name Iráklio was officially adopted in 1913.

man airfield), as well as the only two, small El Greco paintings still on Crete.

E ▶ The **Natural History Museum** (Mon–Fri 8.30am–2.30pm, Sun 10am–1pm; www.nhmc.uoc.gr) lies just west, housed in a former seafront power plant. The museum has interesting displays of flora and fauna as well as sections on how Crete would have looked in Minoan times.

The market on 1866 Street

South of the City Centre
South of Lions' Square is **1866 Street**, nicknamed 'Market Street', which still retains some of the atmosphere of an old bazaar. Here you can stroll past stalls selling fresh produce and souvenirs, or eat at the numerous *ouzeris* that serve the market workers. At the southern end of Market Street is **Platía Kornárou** ◀ **F** (Kornárou Square) where you will find a hexagonal Ottoman pumphouse (now a café) beside the **Bembo Fountain** (Kríni Bémbou), created in 1588 using numerous pieces of architectural spolia, including the torso of a Roman statue.

A short walk northwest from here along the inner arterial road brings you to **Platía Agías Ekaterínis** (St Catherine's Square) where the 19th-century cathedral of Ágios Minás dwarfs two older religious buildings. The small church immediately adjacent is also called **Ágios Minás**, with a splendidly ornate iconostasis – if the church is closed, ask in the cathe-

Museum closure

The Archaeological Museum is closed for major renovation and rebuilding and a temporary exhibition of selected star exhibits is on display in an annexe at the rear of the museum building. The museum is set to re-open sometime in 2012 (some items may change rooms), so check with the Tourist Office (tel: 28102 46299) for the latest information.

dral for the key. Behind these two churches is the 15th-century shrine that gives the square its name: **Agía Ekateríni** (St Catherine). It originally belonged to St Catherine's monastery in the Egyptian Sinai, and served as a monastic school. Today it houses the **Museum of Icons and Sacred Objects** (April–Sept Mon– Sat 9.30am–7.30pm, Oct– Mar Mon–Fri 10am–4pm) – a wealth of art from churches and monasteries across the island, including six large icons by the celebrated Cretan artist Mihaïl Damaskinos.

The Archaeological Museum

Walk southeast from Lions' Square along the pedestrianised shopping street, Dedálou, to reach the city's top attraction, the **Archaeological Museum of Iráklio** (minimum hours Mon noon–5pm, Tue–Sun 8.30am–3pm, until 6pm summer; closed for renovation at the time of writing). One of the greatest archaeological collections in the world, this brings together finds from sites across Crete and from every era of the island's ancient history. Pride of place goes to the best Minoan artefacts.

As the pre-eminent centre of this ancient people, Crete is the main source of information and excavated remains concerning the Minoans. For any other museum this would be treasure enough, yet there are also impressive Greek and Roman artefacts to enjoy. The museum is a must for those intending to visit the ancient sites, since the objects here add life to the now-empty cities and palaces. Note that after re-opening some items may change rooms. To fully appreciate its glories will take at least two hours – the exquisite detail on pottery and frescoes and the fine workmanship in jewellery and everyday tools is breathtaking. Try to visit in the early morning or late afternoon to avoid the large tour groups who arrive at around midday. The 20 rooms are arranged in chronological order, grouping artefacts from each site. Below are some of the highlights of your tour.

Room 1 has the earliest finds, dating from 6000BC (Neolithic and Pre-Palatial periods). Many were found at Móhlos on the northeastern coast. Primitive pottery is on display here – including a rather naive clay bull with an acrobat holding one horn – and finer work such as a stone *pyxis* (jewellery box) incised with geometric patterns and a reclining animal.

Room 2 is the first of two rooms displaying finds from

Ornamental artefact found in the Archaeological Museum

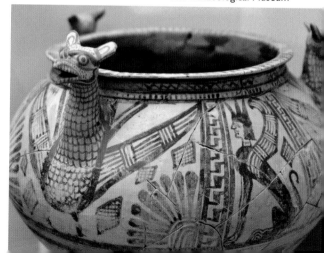

the Proto-Palatial period (2000–1700BC), including the earliest examples of fine Kamáres ware pottery, found in the ruins at Knossos. Fascinating miniature work is also in evidence, with a series of tiny faience plaques depicting the façades of Minoan houses.

Room 3 holds the **Phaistos Disc**, a clay disc 16cm (6¼in) in diameter, imprinted with hieroglyphic and geometric symbols that have yet to be deciphered. All the other finds here were also uncovered at the Phaistos Palace.

Room 4 has finds from the golden age of Minoan society – the Neo-Palatial period (1700–1450BC). Artefacts originated in the palaces of Knossos, Malia and Phaistos and include the superb *rhyton* (libation vessel) carved from black steatite in the shape of a bull's head. The bull was one of the foremost religious symbols of the Minoans and this piece was created by one of the pre-eminent artisans of the time.

The Agía Triáda sarcophagus shows tributes imported from Africa

Room 5 holds objects from the final phase of Minoan civilisation (1450–1400BC). The pottery and stonework is worth studying, but the chief artefacts are the Linear A script fragments incised on thin clay plates and not yet deciphered. Also exhibited are examples of Linear B, which was deciphered in 1952 and is of Mycenaean origin – showing that by the time the tablet was written the Minoans had lost control of the major cities.

Public outcry

In 1979 Prime Minister Constantine Karamalís wanted to loan part of the Minoan collection abroad. The Cretans took to the streets armed, protesting against the removal of their historical art treasures from the Iráklio Archaeological Museum.

Also on display here is a delightful clay model of a Minoan dwelling, complete with roof terrace and tiny windows to keep out the bright sun and fierce Cretan winds.

Room 6 concentrates on tomb finds that date from the Neo-Palatial and Post-Palatial periods. Items on display include beautiful pottery pieces, military artefacts such as helmets and sword handles, and splendid gold jewellery.

Room 7 concentrates on domestic utensils and personal objects found in the palaces and around the *Megara* (royal chambers). These include stone vessels, pottery, hammers and a potter's wheel. There are several intricately carved steatite vessels, including the **Harvester Vase** discovered at Agía Triáda and decorated with a low relief of men at work in the fields.

Room 8 is devoted to the palace of Zakros in the far east of Crete. The 'marine' amphora is decorated with octopuses and Argonauts. A delicate rock-crystal *rhyton* on display here shows the sophistication of both workmanship and personal taste in the Neo-Palatial period. Room 9 has finds from other sites in eastern Crete before room 10 moves on to the Post-Palatial period (1400–1100BC), with pieces decorated in Mycenaean style. Rooms 11 and 12 concentrate on the period between 1100BC and 650BC, including a large collection of gold jewellery. Room 13 contains a number of painted Minoan sarcophagi, many decorated with the images of fish or birds.

Rooms 14 to 16 on the second floor display the finest surviving **frescoes** found throughout the Minoan kingdoms, dating from 1600 to 1400. There are 21 in room 14, and nine in room 15, depicting the enigmatic Minoans at work and play, and their major influences – the bull, other animals and the marine environment. Male figures – presumably out in the sun more – were always rust coloured, while more secluded females were always painted white.

At the centre of gallery 14 is the only stone **sarcophagus** found on the island (at Agía Triáda). Spiral decoration frames scenes of libation and other religious activities. At the far end of the hall you can examine a miniature re-creation of the palace of Knossos, completed according to early hypotheses on its design.

Room 17 houses an exhibition based upon the **Ring of King Minos**, an engraved Minoan gold ring found in 1928 close to the Knossos palace, and long considered to be a hoax before being verified by experts in 2002. Rooms 19 and 20 move on through the Archaic period to the Classical, Hellenistic and Roman eras, with colossal marble statuary gracing the gallery space. The museum has a café and there are several more just across the street from the entrance. Also opposite is the busy main tourist office (Mon–Fri 9am–3pm).

CENTRAL CRETE

Central Crete is the market garden and vineyard of the island, with fertile valleys nestling between rocky mountain ranges. Today it supplies much of the fresh produce for the population, including grapes for the quaffable Cretan country wine. This is not a recent development: it was home to the Minoans, with their most famous palace only a few kilometres away from Iráklio. The Roman capital was also located in this region. Around these important archaeological sites are farming communities quite different in character from the city and the coastal resorts. Spend time exploring these villages for a glimpse of a lifestyle that will soon disappear as the younger generation forsakes rural ways of life.

The Minoan palace at Knossos is Crete's biggest tourist attraction

Knossos

Just 5km (3 miles) south of Iráklio is **Knossos** (daily Apr–Sept 8am–8pm, Oct–Mar 8.30am–3pm), now famed worldwide as the place where Sir Arthur Evans (at that time Director of the Ashmolean Museum in Oxford) found proof that the mythical ancient civilisation of Crete had really existed. Evans named this people the Minoans after their most famous, semi-mythical king – Minos. He began digging in 1900 after buying the site, financing the excavation programme with his own money, and almost immediately struck the first masonry of a huge Bronze Age palace replete with magnificent pottery and other artefacts.

Evans' subsequent attempts to reconstruct areas of the palace have met with intense criticism from other scholars but Knossos (Knossós in modern Greek) is now Crete's premier attraction, and rightly so. Although there is no documented proof, the majority of Cretans believe that Knossos was the site of the famed battle between Theseus and the Minotaur in the Labyrinth below King Minos's palace.

The first palace at Knossos was built *c*.2000BC in the Proto-Palatial era, but this was destroyed by a massive earthquake only 300 years later. Most of what you see here today are the remains of the second palace, built following the disaster. This coincided with a golden age of Minoan society (the Neo-Palatial era, from 1700BC), when the people grew rich through trade, and artistic endeavour was at its peak. The palace expanded continuously through the following years, resulting in a complex of around 1,200 small rooms several storeys high covering over 20,000 sq m (215,280 sq ft). This golden era came to an end in 1450BC, and major fire caused catastrophic damage around 1350BC, but although the palace was completely destroyed, the surrounding town continued to be occupied until the 5th century AD.

The palace was erected around a large **Central Court**, possibly used for public meetings, which now forms the heart of the site. Imagine Minoans at play here as depicted on the pottery and frescoes in the Archaeological Museum in Irák-

Minoan Building Methods

Knossos construction methods were complicated, with light wells illuminating lower chambers, and polythyra, masonry supports to create structural integrity, between which were large wooden doors serving as partitions. Cypress or juniper trunks served as anti-seismic cushioning in walls, and the same wood (often poised upside down) used as columns. Many quarters were semi-subterranean for more comfort in the warm climate, with high windows for ventilation.

The famous 'bull-leaping' fresco shows a daring acrobatic game

lio – acrobats and dancers as well as the famed bull-leapers. Visitors enter past what remains of the **West Court**, used as an entryway to a **West Wing,** where the administrative and religious activities took place. Minoans would walk down the corridor of processions past frescoed walls to reach the *propylaia* (sacred entranceway). A **grand staircase** then led north to the most important official chambers within this wing, its sturdy painted colonnades typical of those found throughout the palace.

The lower floor here houses the **throne room**, with ornate griffin frescoes and a lustral basin for ritual purification. The walls – lined with stone seats thought to have been used by advisers or councillors – would have been decorated with red plaster and an ornamental dado. In the northeastern corner was a crypt where a cache of treasures was unearthed during the excavations.

A staircase by the throne room leads to what Evans

christened the *piano nobile* – a reconstructed upper floor of the west wing. Next to the staircase is the **Tripartite Shrine** where the Linear B alphabetical tablets were discovered.

On the east side of the court, a **grand staircase** leads to the royal chambers or *Megara*, where some of the best preserved rooms can be found. The shallow gypsum staircase is a stunning construction and one of the masterpieces of Minoan architecture. Notice the clever use of lighting wells to illuminate the lowest storeys (there were four in total). The **King's Megaron** is decorated with a simple wooden throne, although the antechamber walls are incised with images of the double axe or *labrys*, so important to the mythology surrounding Knossos. The room is also known as the **Hall of the Double Axes**. The architecture of this room is typically Neo-Palatial in style, with large *polythyra* supporting the roof. It is thought that large wooden doors were fitted between the pillars and that these could be removed to create a *stoa* (open-fronted arcade), if the king wished it. The

Rites and Sacrifices

In the Minoan civilisation, the bull symbolised virility and all natural forces. The walls of the palace of Knossos are covered in paintings and sculptures of huge sacred horns. In the courtyard, young people used to perform an acrobatic game where they had to grab the bull's horns and leap above the animal. Every year, a bull was caught, its throat slit and its blood collected. This sacrifice bound Minoan society and the animal's divine powers to the great cycles of nature. The Mother Goddess was represented by the Snake Goddess's bare breasts, a symbol of fertility. The snake itself was a symbol of reincarnation and healing. The sacred pillar embodied the goddess, while the double-headed axe represented the moon and the double power – religious and political – of the priest-king.

Queen's Megaron has a splendid dolphin fresco lining one wall. On the far side of the site are the remains of the Royal Road leading north to the coast, still in exceptional condition.

Evans made numerous remarkable finds at the site, since it had been covered and left undisturbed following the 1350BC disaster. Pottery intricately painted with marine life, bronze figurines and exquisite jewels – many of these were discovered in the rock-cut tombs of the Post-Palatial period. Yet it is the mundane and simple things that make Knossos so fascinating. Evidence of early water piping, central heating and sanitation show a remarkable sophistication.

Huge jars called *píthi* were used to store grain, oil, wine or water

Towards Gortys (Górtyna)

Other Classical sites lay below Iráklio near the south coast. Take the road southwest to **Agía Varvára**, in a vine-filled valley skirting the looming Psilorítis range to the west. Beyond lies the **Mesará Plain**, a wide fertile valley surrounded by hills and a centre for farming since ancient times. For a pretty drive through the foothills on the north, take the direct road to **Zarós** from Agía Varvára. The scenery is magnificent, with plenty to do locally: idle by the **Votamós lake**, hike the **Rouvás Gorge** just north, or visit the small, frescoed **Moní Vrondisíou** (Vrondísi Monastery) 4km (2½ miles) away on the **Kamáres** road; this was the original home of the Damaskinos icons, now in Agía Ekateríni in Iráklio.

A little bit further, at Vorízia, is the turning for **Ágios**

Fanoúrios (Varsamónero; June–Oct Tue–Sun 8.30am–3pm), another monastic church with vivid 15th-century frescoes. Beyond Kamáres, with its famous cave overhead, the same road continues towards the Amári Valley to the west *(see page 75)*.

To reach the ancient sites drop directly down from Agía Varvára to the Mesará. Near **Ágii Déka** – named after ten saints who were martyred here, and whose purported catacomb is still viewable at the village's west edge – are the ancient remains of **Gortys** (Górtyna), capital of the island during the Roman era (from 67BC) but already an important city in Minoan times.

Gortys is such a huge site – at its height it had a population of 300,000 – that you will see signposts to remains lying amidst olive groves, south of the modern road. By following the signage you will be rewarded with ancient columns resting against olive trees, shards of pottery among the grass, and a governor's palace and amphitheatre to explore.

The fenced main site (daily summer 8am–7pm, winter 8am–5pm) covers only a tiny part of the city, but it protects

Kamáres Pottery

Kamáres vases date from the Proto-Palatial Period, deriving their name from the Kamáres cave on the southern flank of the Psilorítis range, where they were first found. The characteristic features are polychrome paintings on a dark background. Motifs from nature such as spirals and rosettes combine to create a harmonious unity.

Neo-Palatial Period vases of the so-called floral style display leaves or other plant motifs, while marine-style vessels are covered with octopuses, paper nautilus or even coral designs. These vessels were either buried with the dead, given as votive offerings or else used as crockery in the palaces where they were found.

one of the most important archaeological finds on Crete – the **Law Code** dating from the Dorian period, around 500BC. This huge stone tablet was incised with script setting forth the rules on marriage, criminal justice, property and inheritance rights. The tablet is incorporated into the rear of a small Roman **odeion**. The site entrance is dominated by the triple apse of the 6th-century **Basilica of Ágios Títos** (St Titus), all that remains after Arab raiders razed most of the building in AD 825.

The remains of the 6th-century Basilica of Ágios Títos at Górtys

Phaistos

Travel on through the village of Mires to reach **Phaistos** ◄ **5** (Festós), the site of an impressive Minoan palace (daily 8am–7pm summer, 8am–5pm winter). As Gortys rose in prominence towards the end of the first millennium BC, the fortunes of Phaistos declined, though it had been the seat of power for most of southern Crete in Minoan times.

Phaistos is probably the most dramatic Minoan site on the entire island. Its palace is set on top of a rocky knoll with rooms cascading down the hillside. There are sweeping views out across the plain to Mt Psilorítis on the north and the Asteroúsia range to the south. In legend, King Minos installed his brother Rhadamanthys as ruler here. He was known as a wise and honest man consulted by many as an arbitrator.

The layout of the palace is similar to that of Knossos, but here there has been no reconstruction. Instead, the remains of three successive palaces – two from the Proto-Palatial era

The Phaistos disc

and one from the Neo-Palatial era – can be seen, with almost nothing standing more than a metre above the ground. You enter the site down a flight of steps and find yourself in the **west court**, which doubled as a **theatral area**. The remains downhill to the south are of one of the old palaces, just below the walls the new palace. You'll see scant remains of a shrine, with kiln-like storage pits whose function is uncertain. On the east side of the west court, the **grand stairway** leads to the *propylon*, the entryway into the newer palace. The **west wing** – as at Knossos – was chiefly made up of shrines and storerooms, and many objects of ritual use were found during excavations here. Some rooms still house their lustral bowls for ritual purification.

Beyond all this extends the vast **central courtyard** at the southeast corner of the site. From here, you head north towards the royal chambers – two giant *píthi* (large earthenware pots) guard the entryway from the central court. You'll find a peristyle hall here (off limits) and steps leading down to the **King's and Queen's chambers** – both built to make the most of the cooling updrafts of the hillside. The east court was mainly used for practical activities, as there are remnants of a furnace and workshops here – perhaps for copper smelting. They would have supplied the palace with its need for ceremonial or funerary articles.

The **Phaistos disc** was discovered here by workers in 1903 in a tiny, apparently insignificant, clay-walled chamber on the northern edge of the site. The disc, apparently dating from around 1700BC, is covered with a spiral pattern of symbols and geometric forms that have yet to be deciphered. The original lies in Iráklio's Archaeological Museum *(see page 36)* – though plenty of replicas are on sale at the Phaistos site shop.

Agía Triáda and Vóri

Just 3km (2 miles) beyond Phaistos on the same road is **Agía Triáda** (daily 10am–4.30pm), built, archaeologists believe, as a summer palace for the royal court and linked Phaistos by Minoan road. Set on a hillside overlooking the Gulf of Mesará it offered excellent views and cooling breezes, as the sea came much closer in those days. The remains indicate modules of rooms that could work either as a whole or individually – perhaps to accommodate varying sizes of entourage at different times. The west wing housed the royal quarters.

Agía Triáda (original name unknown) was built late in the Minoan era, *c.*1700BC and although it suffered great damage in the cataclysm of 1450BC, it was re-occupied, and a Dorian town was built to one side, its

There are excellent mountain views from Agía Triáda

Mátala beach viewed from one of the famous caves

agora still evident. Since the Minoan settlement was famed for several shrines, scholars have debated that the original palace may have had some religious purpose. Numerous tombs have been excavated on the hillside, and the sarcophagus in the Iráklio museum, finely decorated with cult scenes, was found here. Atop the whole site is the incongruous 14th-century church of **Ágios Geórgios** (always open), with fresco fragments inside.

Just 3km from Phaistos, north of the main road, the traditional village of **Vóri** has clusters of old houses, a central square and an excellent, if spottily labelled, two-storey **Folklore Museum** (daily Apr–Oct 10am–6pm) near the main church. It's an antique-dealers dream of old furniture, weavings and tools touching on every aspect of rural life, from pig-butchery to bootmaking. Look out for eel traps and animal muzzles made of basketry, an all-wood wheelbarrow and the giant smithy bellows.

Mátala to Agía Galíni

A more frequented lunch-and-swim stop is the coastal resort of **Mátala**, about 11km (7 miles) southwest of Phaistos. Here you'll find a good sandy bay lined with tavernas. The waters are well regarded by snorkellers and there are fascinating remains of a barely submerged Roman port. On the northern side are high sandstone cliffs where you will find many large **Roman tombs** (daily Apr–Sept 10am–7pm) cut into the rock. Until the late 1970s, these man-made caves were unprotected and used as free camping spots by legions of countercultural travellers. Today they are fenced-off and cleared out at dusk.

For a calmer, less commercial alternative, try **Léndas** and its long west beach, 23km (14 miles) south from Ágii Déka village beyond the outriders of Asteroúsia. It's too far to fit into most day-outings, so you'll want to spend the night.

Travelling west from the Mesará you'll reach the coastal resort of **Agía Galíni**, its buildings tumbling down a hill to a tiny port from which you can take boat excursions along the coast, the best of these to spectacular **Ágios Pávlos** beach, with a huge dune backing it. North from Agía Galíni the main road leads to Réthymno (see page 71).

The Central Mountains

Heading west out of Iráklio you can take the relatively fast New National Road along the coast, with easy links to the resorts of **Agía Pelagía**, **Balí** and (best) **Pánormos**, or the slower Old National Road, which winds its way inland via Damásta and Pérama. The slow route allows you to explore some of the most rugged and interesting landscapes in Crete, and leads

Crete's caves

There are more than 3,000 caves in Crete – approximately half of all the caves in Greece. This is due to the porous, water-soluble properties of the island's limestone strata.

you back to mythological times when the gods ruled the earth. The **Psilorítis range** dominates central Crete, rising steeply to the chapel of Timiós Stavrós (Holy Cross) on the highest peak – Óros Ídi (Mt Ida) is a distinguished 2,456m (8,056ft) in elevation. In summer the long summit ridge seems almost to touch the clear azure sky; in winter it attracts a mantle of snow and thick menacing clouds, and the foothill villages seem to hang suspended on this swirling grey blanket. Climbing the peak takes around eight hours (round trip) from the Nída Plateau at the base of the ridge, in turn reached on foot from Zarós or Kamáres, or by path or road from Anógia. Between May and June is the best season, when days are long and snow is minimal. Essential equipment includes Loraine Wilson's *The High Mountains of Crete*, which thoroughly documents all alternatives.

The men and women of this region have been among the most stalwart against Crete's enemies, and subject to some of their worst reprisals – none more so than the inhabitants of the village of **Anógia**. The population suffered two bloody occasions under the Ottomans when the village was razed to the ground, and again in World War II. After Cretan and British partisans kidnapped General Kreipe, head of the occupying forces on the island, German soldiers marched into the village, killing all the men and burning houses. Several monuments in the village commemorate these sad events. Through happier times the village has built a reputation for weaving and embroidery – still sold in the lower town – as well as for its musicians (especially the Xylouris clan). This is one place where you will probably see men in their traditional costume of *stivánia* (high leather boots), *vrákes* (baggy breeches) and *saríki* (headband).

Anógia, on a separate secondary route above the old national road, is a popular point of entry to Psilorítis. Follow a paved road out of the top of the village towards the Nída

Plateau, once visited only by shepherds tending their flocks, and its friendly taverna (daily April–Oct, weekends otherwise). From this, it's only a short walk to the **Idaean Cave** (Idéon Andron) where in legend the god Zeus spent his childhood, protected from his father Kronos by fierce, shield-banging warriors, the *kouretes*. Though the cave itself is not very impressive, it held a powerful sway over its ancient people; archaeologists have found votive offerings dating back over 3,000 years.

EASTERN CRETE

This part of Crete offers contrasting landscapes. Some of the longest-established resorts sprawl along the northern coast, while the interior has verdant valleys dividing mountain ranges that were trackless until the 1970s. Here, it is still just

The bare mountains and verdant valleys of eastern Crete

possible to find the traditional rural lifestyle once om-nipresent in the interior of the island. Caves, gorges and ancient sites add to the attraction, and make the east a good location for a combination beach/excursion holiday.

Rowdy Resorts

Heading out from Iráklio you'll pass the airport some 5km (3 miles) away before reaching the beginning of the coastal strip. The New National Road takes you swiftly along, so if you want to explore take the Old National Road where it still exists. This part of the northern coast was the main target of development during the 1970s and 1980s, and it is not to everyone's taste. Large concrete hotels and apartments make up a home from home for many European nationals, with English, German and Dutch menus, satellite football and all the favourite northern European TV programmes. At

Píthi amongst the ruins of Mália's Minoan palace

times it's hard to believe that you are on a Greek island. However, if you want almost nonstop fun, then this is the place for you. Water-parks, bungy-jumping, go-carting, bars and nightclubs – it's all here.

Mália to Neápoli

The development reaches a peak at **Liménas Hersonísou**, although the inland village of **Ano Hersónisos** still has vestiges of its old atmosphere – and some Cretan tavernas. Liménas rivals **Mália** as the island's clubbing capital, famous for fine beaches and also home to the tranquil Minoan **Palace of Mália** (Tue–Sun 8.30am–3pm), in farmland close to the sea around 2km (1 mile) east of town.

Remains under and around the palace indicate Neolithic settlements, although the first palace was built after 2000BC (later than Knossos and Phaistos) and it revealed no Kámaresware pottery from the Pre-Palatial period like that found at the other palaces. Its design is also simpler, with no large halls or fine wall decorations. This first palace was destroyed by an earthquake *c*.1700BC; there are scant remains of it on the northwest of the site.

The new palace centred on an open courtyard with a **west wing** mainly consisting of storerooms and cult rooms. A loggia fronted the square on this wing. In one room a *píthos* was found with a ceremonial dagger inside, and alongside this lay a sword decorated with gold and crystal, leading scholars to conclude that this was a preparation or contemplation room for the king. Up a nearby flight of stairs is an **altar room** with the base of its altar table still in situ.

Further west a *polythron* area with a paved floor is thought to have been the **royal apartments**. Hieroglyphic clay tablets and official seals were found here. Just a little way north of the palace site is the **chrysólakkos** or 'pit of gold', a mausoleum where the much-prized golden bee pendant was discovered among a larger cache of jewels. Archaeologists are now busy excavating the extensive town that surrounded the palace and parts of this – on the palace's northwest flank – can be viewed from an overhead walkway.

Soon after ancient Mália the road turns inland past the town of **Neápoli**, birthplace of Petros Philargos, who, raised as a Catholic, became Pope Alexander V in 1409 – or rather, the Pisan 'antipope', as there were three rival claimants to the papacy at the time. This is the only place on the island were you can try *soumáda*, a sweet drink made from wild almonds. It was capital of Lasíthi district before Ágios Nikólaos, and still marks the start of a scenic road up to the eponymous plateau.

Eastern Crete's prettiest town: Ágios Nikólaos

Ágios Nikólaos

Eventually new and hold highways meet the coast again at **Ágios Nikólaos**, ❹ probably the pleasantest town in eastern Crete. Though Agios Nikólaos – known to many Brits as 'Ag Nik' – suffered from a rash of ugly buildings going up in the 1970s, it has since made an effort to keep its character, and offers a more Greek atmosphere than the Mália/ Liménas Hersonísou strip.

The town sits on the **Gulf of Mirabéllo**, blanketing low hills which rise up from the shoreline. At the centre of town is **Lake Voulisméni**, a 60-metre-deep spring-fed lake where a plethora of pretty fishing boats are tied. Numerous cafés and tavernas line the north and eastern edges of the lake, and you can sit and watch kingfishers swoop for minnows or divers descend to the bluey-green depths.

Life is leisurely in Ag Nik

The south and west sides of the lake are flanked by sheer rock faces and you can climb the steps to the top for superb views over the town – perfect at sunset.

Lake Voulisméni is connected to the sea by an artificial channel. Across the road bridge at its mouth is the main tourist office, and beyond is the main port – where ferries no longer call. From the quay just beyond the bridge, excursion boats ply to local attractions, though it's a very long way to Spinalónga *(see page 59)*.

You won't be able to explore Ágios Nikólaos without climbing a few hills. Shops selling upmarket clothing line the harbourside and Mt Skafianá, leading to Kitroplatía cove. Part-pedestrianised Ikosiogdóis Oktovríou makes for another pleasant stroll towards the central plaza.

The local **Archaeological Museum** (Tue–Sun 8.30am– 3pm) near the top of Konstandínou Paleológou keeps a good collection of Minoan artefacts, presented in chronological order. You may view a sarcophagus with skeleton still in place, and the 'Goddess of Myrtos', an exquisite libation vessel dating from the 2nd millennium BC in the shape of a woman with a long neck and squat body. A later Roman find is the skull from Potamós, decorated with a crown of gold olive leaves. The coin nearby was found between the skull's teeth, presumably the dead man's fare to the ferryman across the River Styx to the underworld.

Eloúnda to Spinalónga Island

Ágios Nikólaos does not have great beaches; Havánia just west of town, and Almyrós 2km (1 mile) south, are serviceable at best. As a consequence much of its up-market accommodation lies north along the coast towards **Káto Eloúnda**. This coastal resort is understated, with a pretty church on the waterfront. You can also head to Spinalónga island from here – a much shorter trip than from Ágios Nikólaos. Don't confuse it with Cape Spinalónga, accessible from Eloúnda via a narrow causeway over an artificial canal.

In the shallows around the causeway are the remains of the Greco-Roman city of **Oloús**, still flourishing during the 2nd century AD, according to Greek geographer Pausanias. It probably sank during tectonic upheavals in the 4th century, which did spare an early Christian basilica (fenced off) inland, whose floor mosaics include frolicking dolphins.

Overnight Sensation

The 2010 Greek television series To Nisi (The Island), based on Victoria Hislop's novel of that name, has been a huge success, resulting in a continuing traffic of Greek visitors to the Spinalónga area. It was shot mostly at Pláka and the hillside village of Páno Eloúnda, as the archaeological authorities did not let Mega Channel's crews use the island itself as a location. The sets at Pláka are now dismantled, but at Páno Eloúnda they have been left as a tourist attraction, cleverly intercalated with the original houses. Wandering the attractive streets, you can see why the village, with its sweeping views, was chosen.

Still further north on the mainland, the tiny coastal resort of **Pláka** has the quickest, cheapest boat transfer (9am–6pm in season) to Spinalónga island, directly offshore. Weekends are very busy – embark before 11am – and take a hat and liquids, as there's no shade or refereshment on the island. **Spinalónga Island** (summer daily 9am–6.45pm, winter by arrangement) is girded with the bastions and curtain walls of the Venetian stronghold, built in 1579 to protect the entrance to the sheltered bay behind; a late Ottoman town on the sheltered, landward side; and the

Spinalónga's former leper colony

leper colony that later occupied it. The fortress was never taken by force; the Venetian garrison remained here until 1715, over 60 years after the fall of Iráklio, and left only after a treaty gave them safe passage. Muslim Cretans in turn retreated to the island when they came under threat from Cretan rebels at the end of the 19th century.

In 1903, the Cretan administrative council decided to establish a leper colony here; whether this was to force the Muslim villagers to leave is debatable, but the disease was rampant on the main island and Spinalónga's position – offshore yet not too remote – was considered ideal for quarantining its sufferers. Initially, the regime was harsh, with victims treated more like criminals than patients; however, conditions improved over the years, thanks to patient activism and a new medication regime after 1948, until the colony was disbanded in 1957. Allow at least 90 minutes to explore the fortifications and the old town. Part of the old market street has been restored, the restored shops house an interesting museum.

Inland to Kritsá

Inland from Ágios Nikólaos are three attractions that fill an enjoyable morning or afternoon of sightseeing. Head out towards the village of Kritsá 12km (7 miles) from town. Before you reach the village itself you'll find a beautiful Byzantine chapel on the right. **Panagía Kerá** (Tue–Sun 8.30am–5.30pm) was built in the 13th century and decorated with superb frescoes of the 14th and 15th centuries. You'll need time, and the guide booklet on sale, to take in every detail of the interior. Although many frescoes are damaged or uncleaned, existing highlights include a 'Presentation of the Virgin' and 'Last Supper' in the vault of the main nave, and the 'Water of Proof' in the south aisle.

Resume your journey toward Kritsá, but don't visit the village just yet. Instead, follow signs 4km (2½ miles) along a side road to **Lató** (free access), the remains of a Dorian city (7th–3rd centuries BC) scattered around two scrub-covered hilltops to the north.

Finally, you can allow yourself to head into **Kritsá** for some well-earned refreshment. This 'traditional' village is perhaps overly touristy for some but it is still very much lived-in and extremely well kept, with brilliant whitewashed walls accented by brightly painted window frames and potted plants. You'll find good tavernas near the old village square – distinguished by its huge plane tree. Famed for its carpet weaving and textiles, you'll see examples hanging from walls and shop doorways in the narrow streets.

Whitewashed walls of mountainous Kritsá

The Lasíthi Plateau

If Kritsá is a good example of a hill-village 'rescued' by tourism, others have seen their rural economy collapse since the 1970s. Travelling inland toward the towering peaks of the **Díkti Mountains** brings you to a region that was isolated from the rest of Crete except by horse or donkey travel until well after World War II. Improved access to the **Lasíthi Plateau** (Oropédio Lasithíou) ironically just accelerated depopulation.

Two main roads climb up to 850m (2,800ft) altitude. From the New Road above Mália you head through the tiny settlements of **Krási**, with an ancient plane tree gracing the main square, and **Kerá**, where you can visit 14th-century **Panagía Kardiotíssis** (Our Lady of the Heart) before proceeding through the dramatic **Séli Ambélou Pass** with its ruined stone windmills.

Or you can ascend from Neápoli on a longer road not used by tour coaches, through the little oases of **Exo** and **Mésa**

Potámi, for a panoramic initial view of the plain and the impressive **Psarí Madára** peak (2148m/7047ft) beyond.

A single road circles the plain, linking all the small communities, though you'll find many of their houses derelict or rented by gypsies, and their shops shuttered since the flight down the mountain. What agricultural activity that still persists is often much delayed lately by heavy spring rains, as the valley floor drains slowly. Potatoes and grain grow on the plateau, with sheep grazing the stubble; orchards (especially apples and cherries) and vines are cultivated on the surrounding slopes. The famous windmills, which used to pump up water in late spring, have now mostly vanished; just a few at the north edge of the plateau are left spinning idly for show, their pistons disconnected and storage tanks empty.

The only village with much life is **Tzermiádo**, almost a proper town. Clockwise from here, stop in **Ágios Geórgios** to visit the three-room **Folklore Museum** (summer only, 10am–4pm), set to expand in the future.

On the southern edge of the plain, 1km above **Psyhró** village where powerful springs nourish a plane tree, yawns the large **Dictean Cave** (Diktéon Andron; daily 8am–7pm), said to be the birthplace of Zeus. Ancient votive offerings left in the cave confirm that it was revered during Minoan times. It is a 15-minute walk (or expensive mule ride) from the parking lot. From the entrance the cave drops precipitously 65m (215ft) into the cavern, which can become very crowded. Try to spot the monstrous face of Kronos here to eat his new offspring Zeus, and the small nipple-shaped stalagmites on which the infant god is said to have suckled.

East to Sitía

Heading east from Ágios Nikólaos, the new road along the northern coast is still in the throes of construction. Follow the gulf intially south to **Ístro** where there is a garland of beaches (best of these being **Voúlisma**), and then east to one of the major ancient sites locally – **Gourniá**, 18km (11 miles) from Ágios Nikólaos (Tue–Sun 8.30am–3pm). Myriad stone walls – foundations for multi-storeyed homes – linked by cobbled streets blanket the hillside. Here more than at any other Minoan site it is possible to envision ordinary people going about their daily business. You may also explore the marketplace and workshops of the artisans.

The palace sat at the top of the hill, its west court housing a sacrificial slab and storerooms for ritual liquids and libations as seen in other

The Dictean Cave is said to be the birthplace of Zeus

Minoan palaces. Gourniá was a large city, stretching down to the coast where it had an important port. Much remains to be uncovered, though there seems little intent to do so. The best overview of Gourniá – excavated by American Harriet Boyd Hawkes in the early 1900s – is from the main road as it rises beyond the archaeological site.

From Gourniá the Old National Road traces a tortuous course, via sleepy hill villages, towards Sitía. The one spot of note actually on the coast, down one of two side roads, is **Móhlos**, now an easy-going resort on a cape despite lacking a beach, but during Minoan times an important site. The Minoan settlement sits on a small island just 150m (480ft) offshore – you can take a boat or swim across to reach it – although it was connected to the mainland 3,000 years ago. A little way offshore to the west is **Psíra**, for which you definitely will need boat transportation to visit the entire Minoan port town.

20 Eventually the northern road drops into **Sitía**, a bustling port town of about 9,000 people – including students at the local geological school and police academy, who keep the waterfront bars and *ouzerís* lively all year.

A Minoan settlement at **Petrás** lies 1km (½ mile) to the east, but the Venetians chose this hillside location, building a fortress – the **Kazárma** – on its highest point. Unfortunately the Turks destroyed the Venetian domestic buildings when they took the town but a network of narrow lanes and stone steps spill down to a waterfront promenade, and these have delightful architectural and lifestyle details to discov-

Tiers of houses rise from Sitía's waterfront

er. Sitía also has a pleasing **Archaeological Museum** (Tue–Sun 8.30am–3pm) displaying finds mostly from Zákros, in particular a large collection of painted *lárnakes* (clay burial chambers), as well as a ceramic wine press and souvláki grill. You'll find it just south of the town centre.

Moní Toploú

Toploú to Zákros

Sitía is the gateway to the far east of Crete. Now sparsely populated, with most villages inland, subsisting on olives and grapes, this region conceals important Minoan sites suggesting that many people lived here 3,000 years ago. For those who want to explore the area, there's plenty of accommodation around Palékastro and at Káto Zákros *(see page 140)*. Surprisingly in this remote part of the island, a procession of tour buses arrives every day from Ágios Nikólaos and beyond.

Many of these are headed for one of Crete's most influential religious institutions, **Moní Toploú** (Toploú Monastery; daily 9am–6pm, Oct–Mar until 4pm), an oasis in an otherwise rather bleak landscape owned almost entirely by the Orthodox Church. Founded in the 14th century, the monastery was built for contemplation, but also for protection against outside threats. Toploú is a Turkish word meaning 'with cannon' – the more correct title for the monastery is Kyriá Akrotirianí – indicating that the abbots were no timorous recluses. Its walls suggest more a fortress than a religious refuge – though even these were not enough to protect it from

Palace of Zákros ruins

being sacked by pirates in 1498. The monastery played a signal role in Cretan uprisings against the Turks – 12 monks were hanged in 1821 – and more recently against the Germans in World War II when it was a safe-house for British soldiers and native partisans. The abbot and several monks were shot in reprisal before the war's end.

The monastery church and museum shelters many treasures, foremost among them the intricate 18th-century icon by Ioannis Kornaros, with 61 miniature scenes based on the Orthodox prayer 'Lord, Thou Art Great'; at its top is a finely wrought Holy Trinity, framed rather bizarrely by zodiacal signs. There are also two galleries of strange and rare engravings, plus illuminated gospels. Sadly, most of the monastery other than the courtyard is now off-limits. In the extensive gift shop, you can buy reproductions of the icon or olive oil produced from the monks' own groves.

Northeast of Toploú awaits one of Crete's natural wonders. Amid arid scenery, a grove of verdant date palms appears, with beyond a swathe of blond sand lapped by azure waters. This is **Váï**, extremely beautiful and correspondingly popular at peak season, when it's absolutely packed. The palms are claimed to have grown from pips spat out by Arab pirates, though the less romantic truth is that they're an indigenous variety *(Phoenix theophrastii)* that have been present here for millennia. If Vái is 'full', retire instead to three less crowded sandy coves 3km (2 miles) north at **Itanos** – there are date palms here too at the southerly cove.

From both Vái and Toploú roads converge on modern **Palékastro** village, with an eponymous Minoan site nearby (still being excavated, free access), overlooking Hióna beach, the ancient port. This is separated by a headland from superior **Koureménos** beach with its windsurfing facilities.

South from Palékastro, the narrower road shys away from the coast, threading villages that are trailheads for great hikes, including through two gorges: the **Hohlahiés canyon**, ending at isolated Karoúmes beach, and the more famous **Zákros Gorge** (better known as the **Valley of the Dead**). Either take about 90 minutes going downhill (2 hours up), with year-round drinking water in the 'Deads' Gorge' (as it's signposted locally). Your reward, at the bottom of Zákros, is a Minoan palace and another long beach with several tavernas.

The **Palace of Zákros** (July–Oct daily 8am–5pm, Nov–June 8am–3pm) sits just behind this strand on flat ground, with its associated town flanking it on the hillside. With its large port, Zákros was well situated for trade with Egypt and Syria. Building began around 1900BC, though these remains are now invisible owing to subsidence. The ex-

Zákros treasures

Zákros, the last Minoan settlement to be excavated (in the 1960s), revealed a wealth of undisturbed artefacts. Tools and ceremonial objects were found just where they were dropped at the time of the great cataclysm, along with the crystal rhyton on view in the Iráklio Museum and a chest containing hundreds of clay tablets inscribed with Linear A script. Archaeologists even discovered an urn with olives preserved through the millennia.

posed, second palace was completed c.1600BC, but the cataclysm of 1450BC saw a sudden abandonment of the city; it was never resettled.

The **west wing** of the palace was mostly devoted to cult practices, with workshops in the south. The **north wing** housed the royal entourage and the main kitchen, while the east was reserved for the royal apartments. Archaeologists discovered treasures in many of these rooms.

One unique aspect of Zákros is the east wing's water feature, behind the royal apartments. The **cistern hall** contains a circular cistern, still full of water, now inhabited by Caspian pond terrapins. Nearby, the ceremonial 'built fountain' has steps descending to a small, square pool.

The Southeastern Coast

At **Xérokambos**, the next shoreline settlement beyond Káto Zákros, the road turns inland to arrive dramatically at upland **Zíros** village; the coast below is either inaccessible by car or unrewarding if you do get to it. At Zíros you might prefer to stay inland, meeting the main road south from Sitía just past **Etiá**, a Venetian-founded village, now abandoned, with a rare and superbly restored Venetian manor-house (Tue– Sun 9.30am–4pm) containing a worthwhile display on life in Venetian Crete. **25**

However you travel, the next reasonable halting-point is **Makrý Gialós**, a low-key if straggly resort with an equally long, gently shelving beach and portside **26**

Ierápetra day trip

From Ierápetra's jetty you can take a trip to Hrissí (Gaïdouro) islet, some 7 nautical miles offshore but plainly visible on the horizon. This nearly flat islet is covered in rare junipers, has at least two white-sand beaches, plus two tavernas for lunch. Excursion boats leave by 10.30am, returning from Hrissí at 4pm.

tavernas. From here west the coast is more populated, with pine trees and little sandy bays (the most scenic of these **Agía Fotiá** and **Ahliá**) en route to Ierápetra, also reachable by a direct (but dull) road across the narrowest point of Crete from near Gourniá.

The mosque in Ierápetra, Europe's southernmost town

 Ierápetra is the fourth-largest settlement on Crete and claims to be the south-ernmost town in Europe. As ancient Ierapytna, it was the last Cretan city to fall to the Romans, who used it as a base for their conquest of Egypt. Today Ierápetra is a thriving agricultural-supply centre, enveloped in ranks of plastic greenhouses, with a resort tacked on to the east almost as an afterthought. The limited list of conventional tourist attractions in the small old quarter comprises a tiny Venetian castle (daily summer 8.30am–7.30pm), an 18th-century mosque with truncated minaret and a small archaeological 'collection' (Tue–Sun 8.30am–3pm) inside a former Koranic school.

West of Ierápetra, the greenhouses have mostly vanished by the time you reach **Mýrtos**, 16km (10 miles) along, a laid-back, slightly 'alternative' resort just beyond the Minoan sites of Foúrnou Korýfi and Pýrgos. Despite German destruction in late 1943 as reprisal for resistance activity, it's a cheerful, welcoming place, almost a proper town, with a long beach and interesting folklore museum (irregular hours). If for any reason Mýrtos doesn't suit, continue 5km (3 miles) west to **Tértsa**, another long beach with the summits of the Díkti range visible overhead. With a car, make the trip west and inland (33km/21 miles) to **Áno Viánnos**, a surprisingly large village in the Díkti foothills overlooking a fertile plain. The big attraction here is a tiny 14th-century **Agía Pelagía** church up the hill (well signposted, always open), with idiosyncratic frescoes from the life of Christ. From here it's easy to continue on into Iráklio district.

WESTERN CRETE

Western Crete offers a diverse range of attractions: two delightful towns on the north coast, unspoiled mountains where you can hike or experience Cretan rural life, tiny south-coast

The Fortezza at Réthymno

villages reached only on foot or by boat. This area is less densely populated than Iráklio district and has more rainfall, making it more lushly vegetated. These contrasts make it a fascinating part of the island to spend a vacation.

Réthymno

Réthymno lies 75km (50 miles) west of Iráklio, one hour away along the New National Road. The site has been set-tled since Minoan times, with Dorian, Greek and Roman re-mains underlying the present town. Venetian rule spawned many of the architectural gems here, although evidence of the Ottoman period also abounds. Réthymno suffered many attacks and sackings over the centuries. Much of the town was badly damaged in the battle for Crete during World War II, although the old quarter survived. Today, a modern tourist district extends to the east, taking advantage of the long sandy bay, but this has not spoilt the old town, a delightful place in which to stroll.

Réthymno has also been the intellectual centre of Crete throughout the ages and is home to the island's most es-teemed university. Annually in July the town attracts artists from across Greece for its Renaissance Festival.

The old town occupies a strategic nub of land jutting out from the long, flat coastline. A huge fortress – **the Fortez-za** (daily mid-March–mid-Nov dawn–dusk) – dominates the site, its walls rising high above the streets on the northwest-ern point . This is considered to be the largest fortification ever built by the Venetians, who completed the task in 1580. The finest views of the walls are from the waterfront prom-enade outside, from where you can appreciate its grand scale.

Once inside, it is easy to imagine a large garrison stationed here, with the ruins of barracks and arsenals scattered every-where. Right at the heart of it is the restored, 1647-built **Mosque of Ibrahim Han**, the largest domed structure in

Greece, now hosting concerts or art exhibits. Despite its strength and dominant position, Ottoman forces made surprisingly light work of taking the fortress in 1646 – they simply landed elsewhere on the coast and invaded the town from the land.

Immediately outside the fortress entrance, the former town jail (closed in 1970) now houses the **Archaeological Museum** (Tue–Sun 8.30am–3pm) displaying late Minoan and Roman finds including clay sarcophagi painted with stylised animals. Walking downhill from the fortress gate brings you to the enchanting **Venetian inner harbour,** now a haven for small fishing craft and excursion boats, guarded by a 19th-century lighthouse at the end of the stone jetty. The harbour cafés where Ottoman Cretans used to socialise over coffee and shared *nargilédes* (hubble-bubbles) have now become somewhat touristy tavernas.

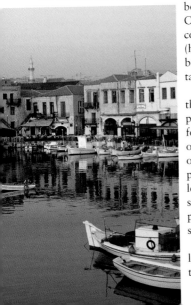

The Venetian harbour

Behind the old harbour the maze of narrow, mostly pedestrianised streets, ideal for strolling, forms the core of the old quarter. The most obvious sight will be shopping opportunities at eye level: craft and jewellery stores create tempting displays, and cotton clothing is swathed across every wall.

However, don't neglect to look behind the merchandise to see Venetian stone lintels

above, or to glimpse ornate
Ottoman *kióskia* (enclosed
wooden balconies) or entire
housefronts draped in
bougainvillaea. At night the
streets come alive with shop-
pers and revellers, and excellent restaurants occupy
some of the old buildings.

Water feature

There are several other
fountains, now dry but
inscribed with elegant
Ottoman calligraphy,
scattered across town. The
easiest to find are alongside
the multi-domed Kara
Pasha mosque and on the
corner of Smýrnis and
Koronéou, below the
Fortezza.

If you exit the harbour
from the southwest, you
cross busy Arkadíou to-
wards the **Venetian Loggia**, built in 1600. It has been rescued from years of dereliction, now housing an up-market
gallery where you can buy excellent copies of museum pieces.
Walk down Paleológou to find the still-flowing **Rimondi
Fountain**. Built in the 1620s, its lion-head spouts have taken
on an aged patina and it looks strangely out of place in this
bustling square.

From here the principal shopping street, Ethnikís Antistáseos, leads south. Turn right onto Vernárdou where you
will immediately find the **Nerantzés Mosque** (Tzamí ton
Nerantzión), a converted Venetian church – something obvious from the north portal – now used as a conservatory
and concert hall. Beyond this the **Historical and Folklore
Museum** (April–Oct Mon–Sat 9.30am–2.30pm, 6–9pm), in
a fine old Venetian mansion, provides an evocative glimpse
of bygone Crete. The upstairs galleries feature embroidery,
weavings, farm and kitchen implements and ceramics.

Ethnikís Antistáseos soon ends at the **Porta Goura**; this
stone gateway, all that remains of the original town walls,
separates the old quarter from the traffic-filled 21st century
just beyond. Across the busy boulevard is the tempting shade
of the **Municipal Gardens**, formerly a Muslim cemetery.

South of Réthymno

The area south of Réthymno is well worth exploring by car, but its major attraction can be visited by public or tour bus. **Moní Arkadíou** **31** (Arkádi Monastery; daily 9am–8pm) lies in the Psilorítis foothills some 23km (14 miles) southeast of Réthymno. It was founded in the Byzantine era, although its present buildings date from the late 16th century, and is revered by Cretans as a nationalist shrine.

In 1866 the Orthodox islanders rebelled yet once more against Ottoman rule. As the attempt failed, hundreds of partisans sought sanctuary in the compound.

Moní Arkadíou, a national Cretan shrine

The Muslims demanded their surrender and, when Abbot Gavriíl (Gabriel) refused, they besieged the monastery.

On 9 November the attackers breached the outer walls to find the Greeks barricaded in a wine depot, where they had also stored their gunpowder. As the Ottoman forces made their way toward this last refuge, the abbot ordered the explosive to be fired. The resulting blast killed hundreds of defenders and attackers, giving real meaning to the battle cry of Crete – 'freedom or death'.

Today, the monastery is a much more peaceful place, although the fateful storeroom remains a charred shell. The Venetian-style church gracing the middle of the compound is one of the most beautiful on Crete. Its façade of yellow sandstone is richly carved with a fine belfry, and mock Corinthian columns dignify each of the twin entranceways.

Southeast of Réthymno lie two valleys leading towards the far coast. The **Amári Valley** is the more easterly and the more exciting, with traditional rural landscapes to explore and dramatic views of Psilorítis as a backdrop. You'll need a car or mountain bike, as public buses or tours here are non-existent, and accommodation scarce. The main valley loop-road leads through small villages, many graced with fine old frescoed churches, and all with memorials commemorating the 1944 German reprisals exacted for resistance operations.

At **Thrónos**, the 11th-century **Panagía chapel** has superb, later frescoes – the shop next door keeps the key (a tip is expected). The adjacent hamlet of **Kalógeros** has the small **Theológos chapel**, with more 14th-century frescoes. **Monastiráki**, southeast of here, offers two more churches: tiny **Aï Geórgi**, at the top of the village, with a fine image of the Panagía Platytéra, and Venetian-style **Arhángelos** (key from café opposite) retains a fresco of the Dormition. East from here, **Platánia** has another Panagía chapel (key from nearby café) with a vivid, nearly complete cycle of frescoes, some unusual – note the rarely shown Angel Gabriel, and St George with a right earring in the Byzantine manner. Going instead anticlockwise from Thrónos, **Méronas** offers the **Metamórfosi chapel** by the school, with well-preserved scenes of St Stephen and the Transfiguration, but the central village church of **Panagía**, with the most complete fresco cycle in the valley, is only rarely opened by the priest.

The second valley to the west leads up to the little hill-town of **Spíli**. Stop to sample the central **Venetian fountain** – a series of 30 kitsch-modern lion-heads spouting crystal clear, cool water from Mt Kédros overhead – before exploring the backstreets.

The South Coast

Beyond Spíli the main road heads east towards Agía Galíni *(see page 51)*, but turn right 6km (4 miles) before Spíli to pass through the dramatic **Kourtaliótiko Gorge** en route to Plakiás and Préveli Monastery on the south coast.

33 **Moní Préveli** (Préveli Monastery; Apr–May daily 8am–7pm, June–Oct daily 8am–1.30pm, 3.30–6pm) is a remote religious community and, like most others, was involved in partisan activities during Crete's struggles for freedom. The fathers helped many Allied prisoners to escape in World War II, while an earlier monastery (Káto Préveli – you pass the evocative but fenced-off ruins en route) was sacked in 1821. Newer Préveli dates from the 17th century and was the richest religious house in Crete during the Ottoman era. Its church contains a splendid iconostasis, considered the best on the island, while in the small treasury museum a gold and diamond crucifix purportedly contains a piece of the True Cross.

Below the monastery, a steep track descends to the car park for '**Palm Beach**', a sandy, stream-fed cove from which the World War II evacuations took place. But it is scarcely worth the effort or parking fee now, as a freak fire in 2010 burnt down most of the palm trees.

In the other direction, west along the coast, minor roads **34** lead to **Plakiás** and beyond. Plakiás is a burgeoning resort situated along a crescent-shaped bay, though better beaches

Mists or Mysteries?

Every year in mid-May local people living near Frangokástello say that they can see the spirits of the dead rebels from 1828 marching around the base of the castle. These *drosoulítes* or 'dewy ones' rise from the morning mists, and meteorologists assure us that they are simply a form of weather phenomena, not phantasms.

flank it at **Damnóni** and **Ammoúdi** to the east, and **Soúda** (with healthy palm trees) on the west.

35 West over the border in Haniá district, the walls of **Frangokástello** can be seen rising behind a sandy beach. This dramatic 14th-century fortress is now just an empty shell – like a set for a film about the French Foreign Legion. The Venetians built it not only to ward off pirates but to intimidate Cretan fighters in the mountains behind. During Ottoman rule Frangokástello was the scene of many critical events, including the capture of the rebel Daskalogiannis in 1770 and the massacre of 700 Cretans in 1828.

Kourtaliótiko Gorge

This secondary coast road ends at Komitádes, just beyond which stands **Hóra Sfakión**, a little port resort that was the main Allied evacuation point after the Battle of Crete in 1941; **36** a memorial commemorates the event. The road veers inland towards **Anópoli**, and coastal points west of Hóra can only be reached by boat or on foot. Boats pick hikers up from the base of the Samariá Gorge, and at busy times rows of tour buses await here to whisk them away. You can take boat trips to inhabited **Gávdos** islet, the most southern territory in Europe, or to nearby **Loutró**, a picturesque village with no vehicular access; alternatively, you can hike west along the E4 trail to Loutró, Anópoli, and many points beyond.

Lake Kourná

From Komitádes, the main road follows the spectacular **Imbros Gorge**, with its rich flora and fauna. This gorge is easier than the nearby Samariá, and you can descend it (takes 2½ hrs approximately) by leaving your car at the village of Ímbros. **Komitádes** marks the bottom, where you can take an afternoon bus or taxi back to your start point.

Réthymno to Haniá

The coastline between Réthymno and Haniá has its share of resorts, although sandy coves are not the rule. An exception is **Georgioúpoli**, with a long, sandy beach demarcated by a river on the west. Its best feature, however, is nearby **Lake Kourná**, the only freshwater lake in Crete, surprisingly large, with idyllic swimming and pedaloes or kayaks to rent.

Northeast from here, via the characterful inland village of **Vámos**, **Kalýves** and **Almyrída** are the busiest spots. All roads emerge at **Soúda Bay**, home of Crete's largest port and one of the Mediterranean's best deepwater anchorages. It is the port for Haniá, with ferry services to Piraeus, while the Greek Navy shares a large base here with NATO. The **British Commonwealth War cemetery** can be found at the head of the bay.

The **Akrotíri Peninsula** flanks Soúda on the north. Here

you'll find Haniá's airport, several small villages and beaches, plus three important monasteries. Seventeenth-century **Agía Triáda** (alias Zangarolón; daily 9am–7pm) is today largely a museum, the most imposing item its Venetian façade, with a small shop selling monastic wine and olive oil. More isolated **Gouvernétou Monastery** 4km (2½ miles) north is a functioning monastery not open to non-Orthodox, but it marks the start of the strenuous, two-hour (round trip) hike down to the evocative remains of **Katholikó**, Crete's first monastery, founded in the 11th century by St John the Hermit. Set on the side of a rocky ravine, it was abandoned during the 17th century in response to pirate raids in favour of Gouvernétou.

As you head towards Haniá, stop at the **tombs of Eleftherios Venizelos** (1864–1936), Crete's greatest statesman, and of his son Sophokles. On this spot, on the orders of Eleftherios Venizelos, the Greek flag was raised in 1897 in defiance of ongoing negotiations amongst the major European powers about the fate of Crete. There are wonderful views across the bay to Haniá, and an adjacent bar from which to enjoy them.

Haniá

The capital of Crete from 1845 until 1971, **Haniá** remains the island's second-largest settlement, and despite extensive modern development at the outskirts, remains an immediately likeable place, currently more prosperous than Iráklio, and one of the few cities where Greeks from elsewhere choose to live. At its heart is a delightful old town replete with Venetian and Ottoman buildings and full of cosmopolitan atmosphere, considered to be one of the most beautiful in the whole of Greece.

The **Venetian harbour** attracts visitors and locals alike. It is huge by comparison with Réthymno's, with outer and inner sections. The waterfront is lined with beautiful medieval buildings and numerous cafés and tavernas, an evening lodestar of attraction. The faded stucco of the harbour buildings takes on a delicate rosy hue as night falls, contrasting with the deep blue sky.

The **Firkás bastion** at the northwest corner of the outer harbour is a Venetian ramparts housing the **Maritime Museum** (Naftikó Mousío; daily summer 9am–4pm, winter 9am–2pm), which displays shells, model ships, maps and naval paraphernalia. Walk through the archway beyond the museum entrance for views east across the harbour from the bastion. Nearby on Theotokopoúlou, the Venetian church of San Salvatore shelters the well-designed **Byzantine Museum** (Tue–Sun 8.30am–3pm), with icons of the Cretan School, jewellery, coins, a floor mosaic and fresco fragments rescued from nearby country chapels.

Sunset over Hania's lighthouse

If you walk down to the sea from here, you can follow partly pedestrianised Pireós inland along the finest surviving section of the old city walls, ending at the massive **Skhiávo bastion**. Staying instead by the sea leads to Neahóra, with its beach and tavernas.

Across the harbour from the Maritime Museum you'll see the impressive buttressed dome of the **Giáli Tzamí** (Shore Mosque), the first mosque built by the Ottomans in 1645 and now an exhibition gallery. Beyond the mosque leads to the inner harbour, with the remains of large Venetian *arsenália* (ship repair yards) – originally 17 lined the water's edge. You can then continue out along the pier to the 19th-century lighthouse at the harbour mouth.

The old quarters extend behind the harbour: narrow alleyways with a mélange of Venetian and Ottoman buildings, a canvas of faded terracotta and ochre stucco dressed with restaurant signs or wares for sale. The shopping here is the most sophisticated on Crete, a legacy of Haniá's days as a bohemian hangout in the 1960s.

Although the streets all seem to run together, there are four recognised sections of the old town. **Tophanás** ('Cannon Hall' in Turkish) behind the Naval Museum, was the Ottoman administrative quarter. Theotokopoúlou, lined with fine Venetian mansions and fashionable cafés, bounds it to the west. At the corner of Zambelíou and Móskhon stands the **Renieri Gate**, built in 1608.

Evraïkí, to the southeast, was the Jewish Quarter during Venetian times. Its small houses awash with pastel hues offer the most shopping and eating possibilities. A synagogue, **Etz Hayyim**, has been restored for visits (Mon–Fri 10am–5pm; Sat evening services), although all of Haniá Jews were deported by the Germans. **Kastélli**, east of the Shore Mosque, was the centre of the Venetian city – as the name suggests there was an older castle here, rendered obsolete when Haniá

Street in Tophanás district

expanded during the 16th century. You'll see a Venetian arcade at the bottom of Agíou Márkou. Kastélli was also the site of Minoan, Greek and Roman Kydonia, the ancient town, partly exposed on Kanevárou.

The easternmost old quarter is **Splántzia**, characterised by whitewashed churches and cobbled alleyways. Platía 1821 forms the core of this neighbourhood, which has more authentic daily life than any other part of old Haniá.

Halídon is a major thoroughfare cutting through old Haniá from north to south. Along here you will find the

F ▶ **Archaeological Museum** (April–Oct Tue–Sun 8am–8pm, Mon 2–8pm, Nov–March Tue–Sun 8.30am–3pm), housed within an old Venetian monastery. The collection spans all eras but is strongest on painted Minoan *larnakes* (clay coffins), Roman statuettes, and Hellenistic mosaics.

G ▶ Nearby is the **Cretan Folklore Museum** (Mon–Sat 9am–6pm), tucked away in a tiny square alongside the Roman Catholic church of the Assumption, essentially an old house crammed with antiques and textiles; reproductions of old embroidery are for sale.

H ▶ **Skrydlóf** (Leather Street), with its mix of traditional goods and trashy souvenirs, heads off Halídon towards the **Agorá**, or covered market, one of Crete's shopping highlights.

West of Haniá

As there are few good beaches near Haniá, many people stay in resorts to the west and simply travel in for the day. **Plataniás** is an excellent option with a lively atmosphere, as are **Agía Marína** and quieter **Geráni**.

Continuing west, **Máleme** is the furthest resort proper; after this, accommodation can be found only in private rooms or small local hotels. The town has a sad legacy, as it was the airfield here (still active) that German paratroopers first seized in 1941, signalling the start of the battle for Crete. Casualties were high for these pioneers, and the **German war cemetery** above the airfield holds the graves of more than 4,000 young men.

Beyond Máleme, the rugged peninsulas of **Rodopoú** and **Gramvoúsa**, jut out from the northern coast, offer plenty of excursions (best to the Goniá Monastery, and Ágios Ioánnis shrine, on Rodopoú, or the lagoon of Bálos on Gramvoúsa). They bracket the port town of **Kíssamos** (alias Kastélli), unremarkable except for its superb **Archaeological Museum** (Tue–Sun 8.30am– 3pm), strongest on Roman/ Hellenistic Kissamos, with a brilliant villa mosaic of 'The Seasons' upstairs. Beyond Kíssamos the broad sandy beach at **Falásarna**, complete with ancient town, and the beautiful lagoon at **Elafónisos** attract numerous day-trippers.

The route from Máleme to Paleóhora on the south coast provides a microcosm of what western Crete is all about. From the wide coastal plain, you climb, then drop, through small villages, the biggest – **Kándanos** – rebuilt after a wartime atrocity and sporting several unlocked, frescoed chapels. Your destination, **Paleohóra**, is a laid-back town with a crumbled Venet-

Two islands

The two islands off Gramvoúsa Peninsula both take its name – Iméri (tame) and Ágria (wild) Gramvoúsa.

ian fort and two beaches – Gialiskári (pebbles) and Pahiá Ammos (long and sandy) embracing it. A part-pedestrianised main street offers every diversion after dark. This is also the end of the line for the south-coast ferries – you can head east towards Hóra Sfakíon.

43 A different road from Kándanos leads to **Soúgia**, an even more relaxed, smaller resort with a huge sand-and-pebble beach (naturists throng the far end) and a variety of walking possibilities, including the hour-plus hike west to **ancient Lissós** through a spectacular gorge.

The White Mountains and the Samariá Gorge

44 The **White Mountains** (Lefká Óri), the island's highest range, with several peaks exceeding 2,000m (5600ft), dominate western Crete. There are almost no villages on its south flank because the mountains rise so abruptly from the Libyan Sea. This is an unforgiving landscape, rugged and stunningly beautiful, with narrow valleys between limestone peaks that wear a mantle of snow until May. Yet these mountains host one of Crete's most impressive, popular and enjoyable excursions –

45 the 16-km (10-mile) walk down the famous **Samariá Gorge**. Starting at an elevation of 1240m (4068 ft), the gorge is the longest in Europe, swollen with melt-water during winter. Only during summer, when the torrent shrinks to a trickle, are people allowed to follow its path. Ancient cypress trees, rare orchids and soaring birds of prey are the overwhelming attractions.

Wild goats

The Samariá Gorge is one of the few places where you might catch a glimpse of the elusive Cretan wild goat known as the *agrími* or *krí-krí*. Built like an ibex, with long curving adult horns, it is sometimes spotted leaping between crags in the White Mountains.

Despite the strenuous nature of the trek – don't set out without sturdy footwear, a hat, sunscreen and a full water bottle – you'll share the narrow pathway with hundreds of other intrepid tourists, which adds to the camaraderie but can spoil the atmosphere if you hoped for solitude. However early you start, you're unlikely to beat the crowds. Most people pay for an excursion that provides a bus ride to the head of the gorge at **Xylóskala** (wooden staircase) and boat transfer from Agía Rouméli, at the southern end, to Hóra Sfakíon where you rejoin the bus. If you travel independently you can take a bus from Haniá to Omalós, just before Xylóskala, and then a

Walking the Samariá Gorge

boat east to Hóra Sfakíon, or west to Soúgia or Paleohóra.

The National Park containing the gorge opens daily at 6am from May to October; after 3pm the main section is closed. Park wardens sell you a ticket, to be surrendered at the other end to ensure that no one is left stranded in the gorge. The descent begins at Xylóskala, in fact a steeply descending path with wooden balustrades for much of the way. With wall-like **Mt Gíngilos** towering above, the stone path drops sharply away in a series of switchbacks, falling 1,000m (3,300ft) in the first 3km (2 miles).

The route becomes less steep once you reach the **Chapel of Ágios Nikólaos**, 4km (2½ miles) in, where there is a picnic area. Springtime freshwater pools are inviting, but swimming

Santorini's capital, Firá

is strictly forbidden. The abandoned village of **Samariá**, with its 14th-century **Church of Osía María** (Mary the Anointed of Egypt), marks the halfway point. People lived here until 1962; now there's only a warden's post and first-aid station. Beyond looms the gorge's narrowest, most memorable point, the **Siderespórtes** (Iron Gates), only 3.5m (11ft) wide but 300m (1,000ft) high. Beyond this, the gorge opens up as it approaches the sea and is much less striking. The final stretch is perhaps the most gruelling as you walk along the shadeless riverbed, but at **Agía Rouméli** you'll be able to enjoy an extremely welcome drink or meal.

EXCURSION TO SANTORÍNI

Although Crete is interesting and varied, you may want to spend a day or two exploring a different Greek island. **Santoríni** (alias **Thíra**) is one of the most beautiful places in the world, and just a couple of hours by fast catamaran from Iráklio. Day trips are offered in every resort.

Arriving by sea allows gradual comprehension of the stunning topography unfolding before you, for Santoríni frames the largest submerged volcanic caldera on earth. A massive eruption of this volcano around 1500BC carried the whole interior of the island high into the atmosphere as ash, changing the climate of the earth for years afterwards. In place of land came water, surging in to fill the 11-km (7-mile) long void and causing massive tidal waves around the Aegean. What remains today is the outer rim of the original circular island. Sheer cliffs up to 300m (980ft) high bound the caldera, and a number of whitewashed settlements nestle along their crests.

Firá

The island capital is **Firá**, perched atop high cliffs in the centre of the long interior curve. Its buildings tumble towards the water below, giving stunning views. A narrow, cobbled trail of 587 steps leads from the town to the small port below, now the domain of a fleet of donkeys that wait to carry cruise-ship passengers into town. There is also a quicker cable car that whisks you up from sea level in a couple of minutes. Most commercial ferries arrive at the new port of **Athiniós** south along the coast.

Firá's narrow, traffic-free alleys make up a shopper's paradise; you can buy anything from a reproduction icon to a genuine Fabergé egg, designer jewellery of the finest quality and designer clothing by the most desirable names. Find a spot for a drink at sunset, which has to be one of the most spectacular on earth.

Among the boutiques and bars are three places of cultural interest. The **Museum of Prehistoric Thíra** (Tue–Sun 8.30am–7.30pm) and the **Archaeological Museum** (Tue–Sun

8am–5pm) display pottery and other artefacts found on the island. The **Mégaron Gýzi Museum** (Mon–Sat 10.30am–1.30pm, 5–8pm, Sun 10.30am–4.30pm), north of the cable-car station, is housed in a beautiful 17th-century fortified house. Most exciting of its varied collections are photographs showing island scenes from before the devastating 1956 earthquake – the last major one to strike Santoríni.

Ía

Firá is beautiful but can get a little oppressive, as visitors crowd the narrow streets. A little way northwest is a smaller town where the pace is a little less frantic. At **Ía** (often written Oia), set on the northern cliffs, the 1956 damage was more sensitively repaired; many homes are still built into the hillsides, and some have been converted into art galleries and shops selling crafts and souvenirs.

Ía has a plethora of small family chapels

Pýrgos, Profítis Ilías and Akrotíri

Aside from the stunning views, Santoríni has many more delights, including 12 villages to visit set among agricultural land. The fertile volcanic soil is blanketed by vines producing the renowned local wine, or plants producing tiny sweet tomatoes. Near the island centre is **Pýrgos** village, with the remains of a Venetian fortress at its core. On a rocky summit to the south stands 17th-century **Profítis Ilías Monastery**. The monastery is only opened for morning or evening liturgy, but it is well worth coinciding with the priest to visit. Pride of place goes to a 15th-century icon of the prophet Elijah. It also has a museum, which conveys a flavour of monastic life. Unfortunately, the hilltop also bristles with antenna and military paraphernalia, meaning outside photographs are prohibited. On the east coast, **Kamári** and **Périssa** have beaches of fine black or red sand – another legacy of volcanic origins – which heat to a ferocious temperature in the summer sun.

In Santoríni's far south is one of the most important ancient sites in the Mediterranean. Near the modern village of **Akrotíri**, a complete city was discovered dating from before 2000BC (closed for excavation works indefinitely, but worth checking to see if it has re-opened). It was totally covered by several feet of ash during the eruption *c.*1500BC but, unlike at Pompeii in Italy, no human remains have been found, leading scientists to believe that the population managed to escape. Since 1967 the site has been painstakingly excavated to give a picture of daily life before the great eruption.

A complex and sophisticated society is being unveiled, probably a colony of Minoan Crete, with organised urban planning, heating, sanitation. Much of the beautiful artwork found here is, for the moment, in the Athens Archaeological Museum, though you can see reproductions at the Thira Foundation Museum in Firá.

WHAT TO DO

SPORTS

Beach Activities

Crete has hundreds of beaches, from tiny coves to lengthy strands. You can choose to spend your day with hundreds of other people, or have the sand all to yourself at a secluded spot. Beaches in the main resorts have well-organised watersports facilities with jet-skis, water-rides, kayaking and parasailing. The biggest are around Agios Nikólaos, Liménas Hersónisou, Mália and Réthymno on the north coast. Head east for excellent windsurfing, especially at Koureménos, near Palékastro.

South-coast resorts tend to be more low-key; beaches are generally smaller, in discrete bays rather than in long stretches of shoreline. You'll find the most diverse range of beach activities at Mátala, Agía Galíni, Plakiás, Mýrtos and Paleohóra.

Váï, in the far northeastern corner, is considered the most exotic beach on Crete, and, like Elafónisos in the far southwest, gets extremely busy in summer. Most remoter beaches, where you can find some solitude, are at the end of steep tracks which may or may not be paved.

Walking and Hiking

Walking in Crete is amply rewarded with small remote villages, hidden churches and a rural lifestyle to explore. Itineraries can range from short easy walks to steep mountain ascents; however, it's not advisable to head into the high peaks without good maps and a trekking guide. The best all-in-one title is Loraine Wilson's *The High Mountains of Crete* (Cicerone), with reliable route descriptions and sketch maps.

Crete offers a wealth of opportunities for beach activities

Rugged walking country: the Valley of the Dead at Zákros

The European long-distance E4 trail threads the island from Kíssamos to Káto Zákros, and full (or partial) traverses have become increasingly common. Gorge walks are also popular; the Samariá is the busiest and the longest. Others include the Imbros and Askífou Gorges near Samariá, the Rouvás Gorge near Záros on Mt Psilorítis, and the Hokhlahiés and Zákros canyons on the east coast. The peninsulas off the northwest coast offer dramatic and interesting walks, for example the trek to Agios Ioánnis chapel on Rodopoú. Akrotíri is not as rugged as Gramvoúsa and Rodopoú, but does have an excellent route between Agía Triáda and Katholikó monasteries. Other rewarding short itineraries are around Soúgia (southwest coast).

You'll find local agencies arranging organised hiking tours in many resorts, and plenty of overseas specialist companies offer organised hiking holidays in Crete.

Cycling

Mountain-biking and bicycle-touring are becoming increasingly popular. Remember, though, that Crete is extremely mountainous. In some resorts, especially in the west, local companies offer easy cycling tours, with a bus following behind to get you up the hills.

Diving and Snorkelling

The waters around Crete, especially off the southwest coast, offer interesting diving and snorkelling opportunities for water-lovers with all levels of experience. Although the Mediterranean is overfished, and its waters not warm enough to support colourful tropical fish, there are still numerous species to spot in the rocky shallows, including octopus that make their homes in crevices. The remains of many ancient sites lie just off the coast.

The Greek government is anxious to preserve submerged archaeological treasures, so diving is strictly regulated, and permitted only with a qualified dive company that will oversee underwater activities.

If you have never tried scuba-diving before, each dive centre is licensed by the government to offer training in addition to dive supervision for qualified divers. The basic qualification, an Open Water Certificate, normally takes five days to complete. Many centres also offer introductory sessions.

Learning to dive

If you are learning to dive, make sure that you choose a dive centre affiliated with one of the major certifying bodies: PADI (the Professional Association of Diving Instructors), BSAC (British Sub-Aqua Club) and CMAS (Confédération Mondiale des Activités Sub-aquatiques) are the most common.

ENTERTAINMENT

Numerous fairs and festivals take place throughout the year. Local tourist offices will have details of what's happening during your stay on Crete. Each community celebrates its patron saint's day, when the saint's icon is usually paraded through the streets. After a solemn religious service, the rest of the day (or evening) is given over to revelry. These are the best places to see traditional Cretan dances and live music, and to join in with local people having some fun.

Music and Dance

For many, Greek music and dance is inexorably linked to the film *Zorba the Greek (see box below)*, with Anthony Quinn performing the *syrtáki*, an amalgam of several traditional dances, accompanied by the *bouzoúki*. Taverna owners' habit of playing this tune at high volume does a great disservice to the rich and venerable music tradition of Crete, where traditional instrumentalists and singers are held in high regard.

Musical rhythms throughout Greece are very different from the 'four beats to a bar' that characterises western music, and can be difficult for foreign would-be dancers to follow. Song lyrics, usually sung by men, refer not only to the hard life of shepherds, farmers and fishermen, but also touch on love (especially unrequited) – an element of sentimentality rarely expressed directly at other times.

Zorba's Dance

The film *Zorba the Greek* brought international fame to author Nikos Kazantzakis' 1946 novel. Michael Cacoyannis, a Greek film-maker of Cypriot origin, made the film in 1964, with Anthony Quinn in the leading role as Alexis Zorba. His famous *syrtáki* dance scene dismayed the islanders as it is not a genuine Cretan dance at all. The indigenous *pendozáli* proved too difficult for the American actor to learn, so soundtrack composer Mikis Theodorakis came up with a simple but danceable melody in its place. The hordes of tourists who later came to Crete asked to see a dance that did not actually exist, but hoteliers and the music industry moved quickly to oblige them. *Syrtáki* is performed at today's 'Cretan evenings', and recordings of the catchy tune are available everywhere.

Crete's main traditional musical instrument is the *lýra*, a three-stringed lap fiddle, played upright. It is usually accompanied by the *laoúto*, a long-necked, fretted development of the Arab *oud* (lute), and sometimes the *askomandoúra* (bagpipes with two chanters but no drone). These instruments typically accompany *mantinádes*, sung rhyming couplets. Some of these have been passed down through generations of Cretans, but many are improvised on the spot. The men of the western Lefká Óri range sing sparsely accompanied songs, the *rizítika*, elegies for battles

A tradition of dance

and heroic personages. The mountain men also have their distinctive, martial *pendozális* dance; in Réthymno and other coastal towns, the pan-Aegean *soústa* is common.

Chanting epic poetry is also a long-standing Cretan tradition. The 17th-century epic *Erotokritos*, written by Vitsentzos Kornaros in local dialect, is the most popular of these, having inspired many modern Greek poets, and has been set to music repeatedly.

Good places to see traditional music include the mid-summer festivals of the largest towns (see page 103). Throughout the island, larger hotels stage weekly 'Greek nights', or organise excursions to events at village tavernas. The music and dance is usually of a high standard, although surroundings are hardly authentic. More atmospheric is Café Kriti (Lyrakia) at Kallergón 22 in Haniá's old town, with danceable music provided by itinerant musicians (Wed–Sun 8.30pm onwards, tel: 28210 58661). An intimate venue for all kinds of acoustic music (including Cretan) is the first-floor bar of the Pagopoieio, on Platía Agíou Títou in central Iráklio (tel: 2810 346028, www.pagopoieion.gr).

In far eastern Crete, near Palékastro, another unlikely but wonderful acoustic stage is Maridatis (tel: 28430 61055, www.maridatis.gr), a musical taverna behind the eponymous cove, featuring named Greek performers every Friday and Saturday (July–Sept).

If you want to study music seriously, there's an excellent museum and performance centre in Houdétsi village, near Iráklio (see www.labyrinthmusic.gr for details), they usually have an excellent August festival of both Greek and foreign music. More casually, patronize the excellent Aerakis CD shop at Dedálou 37 in Iráklio (tel: 2810 225758, www.aerakis.net), which specialises in local musicians.

SHOPPING

Shopping is one of the delights of a visit to Crete; souvenirs abound in all quality and price ranges. Most resort souvenir shops cater to mass-market tastes, but you can find locally produced goods, and the narrow streets of the old towns provide hours of browsing. Marked prices can be flexible, particularly in tourist shops and at the beginning and end of the season.

Textiles

Sheep's wool and goat's hair have always been used to produce handwoven material (*yfandá*), clothing and interesting carpets or throw rugs. Today, machine-produced items far outnumber handmade pieces. Brighter colours often indicate

synthetic dyes, whereas traditionally made items show
the muted earthy colours of
natural dyes. The price dif-
ferential will also indicate
which is which.

Dolphins and fish are
popular themes, as are
stylised images of Greek
gods. You'll find particularly interesting ranges in Kritsá and Anógia, and also on
the approach to the Dictaean
Cave in Lasíthi and in shops
in Haniá. The only remaining traditional loom-weaver
in Crete is Mihalis Manous-
akis, at his shop Roka (Zambelíou 61, tel: 28210 74736)
in Haniá's Venetian outer
port. Tophanas, nearby at

Souvenirs for sale in Iráklio

Angélou 3 (tel: 28210 72058 or 6978 703592), is a treasure-
trove of antique Cretan textiles, but they don't come cheap
and the owner admits he has to bulk up the stock with imported items.

If rugged textiles don't appeal, then you'll also find beautiful embroidered items such as cotton and linen tablecloths
and napkins. Again the hand-embroidered pieces are the best
and most expensive, but this skill is a dying art, so good examples are becoming harder to find. However, you will have
plenty of everyday tablecloths to choose from in markets and
the main tourist centres. The Centre of Traditional Folk Art
and Culture, at Skoufón 20 in Evraïki, Haniá, sells some remarkable modern embroidery.

Leather Goods

Leather remains extremely good value in Greece, with bags, purses, luggage and belts found in abundance – try Skrydlóf Street in Haniá to begin comparing quality and prices.

Traditional leather sandals (flat soles with leather straps) are still sold in the streets of Réthymno and Haniá. There is also a workshop at Kritsá, but nowadays modern mass-produced fashion shoes seem to be displacing them. You can also purchase a pair of *stivánia*, Cretan shepherd's boots – almost knee-high black leather with thick soles. They are guaranteed to last decades and, judging by the number of well-worn pairs on feet in the hinterland, that certainly seems true. These are handmade to order, will take about a week to complete, and are accordingly expensive.

Knives and Antiques

Hand-forged Cretan knives are made by various knife-makers, especially in Réthymno and Haniá; stainless-steel blades are fitted to olive-wood, bone or horn handles, and are usually inscribed with an appropriate *mantináda* (rhyming couplet). One of the best shops in Haniá's traditional knife-making district (Maherádika) is O Armenis at Sifáka 29, owned by Apostolos Pakhtikos. Just a few paces away at Sifáka 18 is Crete's best antique outlet, Tzangarakis, specialising in reasonably priced copper items.

Clothing

In terms of warm-weather fashions, you should be able to buy everything you need in Crete, so don't worry if you can't find appropriate summer clothes or swimwear at home before you leave. Early and late in the season you can buy good-quality cotton sweaters to guard against evening chill.

Stores in the big towns – including chain outlets like Zara and Benetton – stock major designer labels. Prices can be high by EU standards; summer sales run from late July.

Edibles

Olives and olive oil are obvious souvenir choices; the quality of both is considered among the best in Greece. Particularly good are extra virgin coldpressed oils from Sitía, Toploú and Agía Triáda.

Honey is also one of the prime staples of the Cretan diet; wild herbs and flowers on the hills impart a wonderful flavour.

A variety of herbs are collected and dried for you to take home and use in your cooking. Basil, thyme and oregano are the most common, though you can also buy mixed sachets. Dittany (*díktamos*) herb has been used to make tea on the island for centuries; sage (*faskomiliá*) and mountain ironwort (*malotíra*) are also popular tea-bases.

Olives ripening on the tree

Art and Icons

Artists flocked to Haniá from the early 1960s onwards, and this has left a legacy in the quality of work on sale here (and to a lesser extent across Crete). There are several galleries displaying work by local and international artists in the narrow alleyways of the Evraïkí quarter. A more Greek art form is the icon or religious portrait, usually of a saint or apostle, and lie at the heart of Byzantine or Orthodox worship as they form a focus for prayer. For centuries icons were popular souvenirs of the European Grand Tour or religious pilgrimage. However, modern production methods using gaudy synthetic colours saw them lose favour. In recent years there has been a rebirth in icon-painting using traditional methods, both for church renovations and for commercial sale. This time-consuming work is exquisite and correspondingly expensive. Most monasteries on Crete create certified copies of their most celebrated icons, and you can also find them in jewellery shops in the towns.

Jewellery

Both gold and silver are sold by weight, with relatively little extra cost for workmanship, so they represent good value for money. Ancient Minoan patterns are common with necklaces, bracelets and rings in matching sets. You can also find items featuring precious and semi-precious stones. The House of Amber, Kondyláki 13, Evraïkí district, Haniá, specialises in amber 'worry beads' (*kombológia*). However, you don't need a large budget to buy trinkets; popular street jewellery uses leather, semi-precious stones and crystals.

Buying antiques

There are some excellent copies of museum pieces for sale. These will come complete with a certificate of authentication, which you may need to show to customs as you depart. If you want to buy a genuine antique (anything produced before 1821), you will need a permit to export it. Always consult an expert when you do this in order to avoid subsequent problems.

Pottery and Ceramics

It's not surprising – given the importance of pottery throughout Crete's history – that it is still a significant industry. Pieces come as small as a ring holder to huge gar-

Local ceramics for sale in Haniá

den pieces. Both unglazed and glazed styles are available; most notable of these is the bright-blue glaze of Haniá ceramics. Traditional designs abound, including marine themes, Minoan designs and Classical Greek imagery. Modern abstract pieces can also be found, particularly in Haniá, where avant-garde potters stock galleries. At Margarítes you can watch the potters at work and buy from their workshops.

Olive-Wood Items

Annual prunings and heftier trunk wood are fashioned into a myriad of useful or decorative items: cutting boards, cooking utensils, napkin rings, candle holders. Cutting boards should ideally be one piece and not made of glued-together sections. Large pieces require long seasoning and are hard to work, thus don't come cheaply. One particular workshop to recommend, off the beaten track, is Nikos Vostakis (tel: 28330 41061) in Vyzári village off the Amári valley.

CHILDREN'S CRETE

Crete isn't all about museums and ancient sites – there's also lots of fun to be had for younger members of the family. Greek society is very family-oriented, and children will be very welcome at tavernas and cafés.

Beach activities are well-organised on the northern coast, with all types of watersports and rides. The best sandy beaches are at Mália, Réthymno, Georgioúpoli and Vaï. South-coast resorts such as Plakiás, Paleohóra and Mátala have good beaches and plenty of snorkelling opportunities for older children. Water-parks near Haniá (Limnoupolis, www.limnoupolis.gr), Iráklio (www.watercity.gr) and Liménas Hersonísou (www.acquaplus.gr) will keep them occupied for hours.

A horse-and-carriage ride through the streets of Haniá is a great treat and gives young children a good vantage point. Trips along the coast in colourful *caïques* offer the chance to enjoy a cooling breeze and an alternative view of the island. Castles such as the Koúles in Iráklio, Réthymno's Fortezza and Frangokástello allow imaginations to run wild.

Children might like to take a carriage ride in Haniá

The rural lifestyle of the interior – watching goats filing past, or donkeys working hard for their owners – will delight urban children. Older children should also see gorge walks as exciting adventures. If you want to spend some time apart from your kids, many larger hotels have children's clubs and crèches for toddlers.

Calendar of Festivals

Each Cretan community celebrates its own saint's day (often more than one), there are too many such celebrations, called *panigýria*, to list here. Below are the major events occurring across the island.

6 January: *Theofánia* (Epiphany). Youths dive for a crucifix thrown into harbours.

February/March: Street carnivals with floats and masquers in Réthymno and Iráklio on the two weekends before Lent.

March/May: Easter. *Epitáfios* processions on Good Friday; effigy of Judas burned on Saturday; in churches the sacred flame passes to worshippers' candles Saturday midnight; on Sunday a lamb is barbecued.

23 April: Ágios Geórgios (St George), patron saint of shepherds; sheep-shearing festival in Así Goniá.

20–27 May: Battle of Crete commemorated at Máleme and Haniá.

23–24 June: St John the Baptist/Midsummer's Eve, celebrated with bonfires which are leapt over.

Late June: Casa dei Mezzo Music Festival. Classical chamber concert series at Makrý Gialós and Etiá.

July: Renaissance Festival of dramatic and musical performances at Réthymno.

July–August: Kornaria Cultural Festival in Sitía,

July–Sept: Iráklio festival, with theatrical and music events.

15 August: *Kímisi tís Panagías* (Dormition of the Virgin). Celebrated throughout Crete, at churches dedicated to the Virgin.

25 August: Ágios Títos (St Titus, patron saint of Crete). Procession in Iráklio.

29 August: Ágios Ioánnis (John the Baptist). Pilgrimage on foot (4-hr round trip) to Ágios Ioánnis chapel on the Rodopoú Peninsula.

28 October: *Óhi* Day. Celebrates Greek defiance of Italians in World War II.

7–9 November: Commemoration of the Arkádi Monastery explosion with a fireworks display.

EATING OUT

Greek food has always incorporated local and seasonal ingredients at the peak of their flavour and freshness, served raw or cooked simply – grilled, flash-fried or slow-baked. Since Crete was settled several millennia ago, its people have relied on staples like olive oil, fragrant herbs, wild greens, seafood, lamb or goat meat, and an abundance of fresh garden vegetables, fruit, pulses and nuts. Combine these with more recent Venetian and Ottoman influences, and you have an interesting cuisine. The island shares many recipes with the Greek mainland, but it also has numerous ingredients and dishes found nowhere else.

Today, the traditional Cretan diet is considered to be one of the healthiest in the world, and it is well worth following locals to the better eateries to try it.

Where to Eat

Crete has a range of eateries specialising in certain types of food and drink. Although the boundaries between them are blurring, the following explains what you can expect to find.

A *psistaría* offers charcoal-grilled meat dishes, plus a limited selection of salads and *mezédes*. The *tavérna* is a more elaborate eatery, often family run, offering the pre-cooked, steam-tray dishes known as *mageireftá*, as well as a few grills and bulk wine. A *psárotaverna* specialises in fish and seafood.

An *ouzerí* purveys not just that quintessentially Greek alcoholic drink, but also the *mezédes* dishes that complement it – *oúzo* is never drunk on an empty stomach. Octopus, olives, a piece of cheese or a platter of small fried fish are traditional accompaniments, but there will be various other platters to choose from. A *mezedopolío* is a more elaborate *ouzerí* where food takes precedence.

The *kafenion* is the Greek coffee shop, traditionally a men-only domain, and still so in the inland villages. Usually very plainly decorated with old tables and chairs, they are the venues for political debate and serious backgammon games.

When to Eat

Tavernas in resort areas may offer a full English breakfast, as well as lunch and dinner. Typically, Greeks don't take breakfast – a coffee and *friganiés* (melba toast) or a baked pastry is about as much as they'll indulge in. Lunch is eaten between 2.30 and 4pm, followed by a siesta before work begins again

The *kafenion* is the traditional meeting place for men

at 5.30pm. Dinner is eaten late, usually from 9.30pm onwards, and some establishments take last orders as late as midnight. Sunday evening and part or all of Monday are usual taverna closure times.

WHAT TO EAT

You will usually be given an extensive menu; items currently available will have a price pencilled in beside them. But your waiter is the most reliable guide to what's on that day; menus are mostly to check that the taverna is within your budget– especially for typically pricey items like meat or fish.

A selection of appetising *mezédes*

All restaurants render a cover charge. This includes a serving of bread and is usually no more than €1 per person – if you can, try *paximádia* (the traditional Cretan dry bread) or *dákos* (barley rusks), the latter often the basis of a popular salad (called *koukouvágia* in Réthymno district).

Appetisers

Carefully selected appetisers (*mezédes*) can constitute a full meal on Crete. Shared by the whole table, they're a fun and relaxing way to eat.

The most common appetizers are *tzatzíki*, a yogurt dip flavoured with garlic, cucumber and mint; *dolmádes*, vine leaves stuffed with rice and vegetables – rarely mince – which can be served hot (with *avgolémono* sauce, made of eggs and lemon) or cold (with yogurt); *taramosaláta*, cod-roe paste blended with breadcrumbs, olive oil and lemon juice; *gígandes*, large beans in tomato sauce; *keftedákia*, small meatballs flavoured with spices; *kalamarákia*, deep-fried squid; *plevró-tous*, oyster mushrooms and *tyrokafterí*, a spicy cheese dip.

Saganáki is yellow cheese coated in breadcrumbs and then fried, while *féta psití* is feta cheese wrapped in foil with garlic and herbs and baked. *Kalitsoúnia* are little turnovers stuffed with greens or soft cheese, the latter often served with honey.

Cretan specialities include *volví skordaláta* (wild pickled narcissus bulbs with garlic), *marathópitta* (fried fennel pie), *apáki* (lean cured pork) and *sýnglinos* (a fattier cured pork). Wild greens like *stífnos*, *stamnagáthi* (spiny chicory, often paired with meat) and *askolýmbri* (golden thistle) are especially popular. Greek salad or *horiátiki saláta* (literally 'village salad') consists of tomato, cucumber, onion, green peppers and olives topped with feta cheese. Cruets of olive oil and wine vinegar to dress it are found with other condiments on the table.

Soups are winter staples, but availability is more limited in summer. *Psarósoupa* (fish soup) is a standard on many seafood restaurant menus. *Fakés* (lentil), *revýthia* (chickpea) or *fasoláda* (bean) soups are excellent meatless options.

Fish and Seafood

At fish tavernas, the day's catch is displayed on ice inside a chiller case for you to make your choice, which will be weighed, uncleaned, before cooking – check prices as seafood is almost always a relatively expensive option. If the seafood is frozen or farmed (likely from June to September), this must be stated on the menu – though often only in the Greek language column, or simply with an asterisk.

Larger fish is usually grilled or baked, and smaller fish fried; all are served with fresh lemon wedges or *ladolémono* (olive oil with lemon juice). The most common species of fish are *barboúni* (red mullet), *xifías* (swordfish), *koliós* (chub mackerel) and various breams. More elaborate seafood dishes include

Fried fish platter

ktapódi krasáto (octopus stewed in a red wine and tomato sauce); *soupiá* (cuttle-fish with spinach rice); or *garídes saganáki* (prawns in a cheese sauce).

Meat Main Courses

Meaty take-away snacks include *gýros* (thin pork slices cut from a vertical skewer and served with garnish and *tzatzíki* in pitta bread), or *souvláki* (small chunks of meat cooked on a skewer). Sit-down barbecued dishes include whole chickens, *loukánika* (sausages, the best are from Sfakiá district), sides of lamb or *soúvla* (rotisseried pork), all cooked to melting perfection. *Brizóla* – pork or veal – is a basic cutlet; lamb or goat chops, however, are *païdákia*. Roasted or barbecued lamb is the traditional post-Easter fare. Boiled goat (*gída vrastí*) is also a very popular village dish, often served with a side of *gamopílafo* (sticky white rice).

Stews include *kléftiko*, (braised lamb with tomatoes), *stifádo* (braised beef with onions) and *giouvétsi* (meat baked with lozenge-shaped *kritharáki* pasta) – each comes in a small clay pot that keeps the contents piping hot. *Tsigaristó* is a less elaborate stir-fry of lamb or goat chunks with vegetables.

Greece's most famous slow-cooked oven dish is *mousakás* – successive layers of aubergine (eggplant), potato slices and minced lamb topped with a layer of béchamel and seasoned with nutmeg; good restaurants make a fresh batch daily. *Pastítsio* is another layered oven-baked dish of macaroni, meat and cheese sauce.

For a hot meatless dish, *gemistá* are tomatoes, courgettes or peppers stuffed with herb-flavoured rice (though meat stock may be used). Alternatively *melitzánes imám* (eggplant baked richly with tomato, garlic and oil) is reliably vegetarian, as is *briám* or *tourloú* (ratatouille).

Cheeses

Most Cretan cheeses are made from cow's, ewe's or goat's milk, or often blends of two milks. The best-known cheese is *féta*, featuring in every Greek salad or served alone garnished with olive oil and oregano. *Graviéra* and *kefalotýri* are the most common hard-grating cheeses, varying in sharpness; there are also many sweet soft cheeses such as *manoúri* and *anthótyro*. *Stáka* is clotted cream made from goat's milk.

Dessert

Most tavernas bring a plate of fresh seasonal fruit *(see box)* as a finale to your meal; for something more substantial, a *zaharoplastío* (cake shop) dishes out some decadent sweets,

Snail Delicacies

Snails (*hokhlí*) from Crete are much prized throughout Greece. They are eaten fresh only during the warmer months, when they are dormant, or immediately after rain when they emerge, but are also served from frozen at Lent. *Hokhlí* are prepared in reputedly 40 different ways, including: scalded in salted water; stewed with potatoes and courgettes; fried in rosemary, garlic and oil; or, best of all, cooked with tomatoes, potatoes and thyme, in a dish called *egíni*.

one of the more enduring legacies of the Ottomans: *baklavás*, layers of honey-soaked flaky pastry with walnuts; *kataïfi*, 'shredded wheat' filled with chopped almonds and honey; *galaktoboúreko*, custard pie; or *ravaní*, honey-soaked sponge cake. If you prefer dairy desserts, try yogurt with local honey, or *ryzógalo*, cold rice pudding at a *galaktopolío*.

WHAT TO DRINK

Greek wine-making goes back over three millennia; quality has risen dramatically in recent decades. But owing to limited export – many wineries produce under 20,000 bottles annually – you're unlikely to have heard of even the best labels. Cretan wine in particular was celebrated throughout antiquity, only losing favour in relatively modern times.

Cretan wine is also available in bulk – *hýma* or *varelísio*. Red, white or rosé are offered in full, half or quarter-litre measures, either in colourful aluminium vessels *(katroútza)* or in glass flagons. Quality varies considerably across the island; if in doubt, order a quarter-litre to start with as a test, and a can of soda to dilute it.

Oúzo is taken as an aperitif with ice and water; a compound in its anise flavouring makes the mix turn harmlessly cloudy. Cretans favour their own spirit *rakí*, distilled like *oúzo* from grape pressings but unflavoured. Alcohol strength of either ranges from 40–50 percent. It is the least expensive tipple on the island,

Favourite fruits

Fruit platters after meals typically feature watermelon or Persian melon in summer; grapes or pears in autumn; sliced apples with cinnamon much of the year; and citrus or maybe even some strawberries in early spring. Greece imports just a few temperate fruits from Italy or Spain and relatively little tropical fruit, so this is pretty much the full repertoire.

often literally cheaper than bottled water; many tavernas offer a small *karafáki* (tumbler) of it on the house at the conclusion of the meal.

Nearly a dozen beers are produced in Greece, local labels include Fix, Vergina (reckoned to be the best two), Alfa and Mythos.

Non-Alcoholic Drinks

Hot coffee is served *ellinikós* or 'Greek' style, served in small cups. It will automatically arrive *glykós* (sweet) unless you order *métrios* (medium) or *skétos* (without sugar). Don't drink right to the bottom as that's where the grounds settle. Instant coffee *(nes)* has made big inroads in Greece; more appetising is *frappé*, cold instant coffee, whipped up in a blender.

A local favourite

Soft drinks come in all the international varieties, while juices are usually from cartons rather than freshly-squeezed. One of the most refreshing drinks is Cretan mineral water, fresh from mountain springs.

Dittany *(díktamo* or *érondas)* herb is sold across Crete. It is used to make an infusion claimed to have beneficial effects on a host of ailments. You won't find it on many restaurant menus but you may be offered it if invited to a Cretan home.

TO HELP YOU ORDER

Could we have a table?	**Boroúme na éhoume éna trapézi?**
Could we order, please?	**Na parangiloúme, parakaló?**
a half litre	**misó kilo**
I'm a vegetarian	**Íme hortofágos**
Bon appetit	**Kalí órexi**
Cheers!	**Giámas!**
The bill, please	**To logariazmó, parakaló**

MENU READER

arní	lamb	**moskhári**	beef
avgá	eggs	**oktapódi**	octopus
barboúni	red mullet	**pagotó**	ice cream
býra	beer	**(pagoméno)**	(chilled)
domátes	tomatoes	**neró**	water
eliés	olives	**piperiés**	peppers
fasolákia	runner beans	**psári**	fish
froúta	fruit	**psitó**	roasted
gála	milk	**psomí**	bread
garídes	small shrimp	**revýthia**	chickpeas
gemistá	stuffed	**rýzi**	rice
hirinó	pork	**saláta**	salad
hórta	boiled greens	**soúpa**	soup
katsíki	goat	**spanáki**	spinach
kotópoulo	chicken	**sta kárvouna**	grilled
kounélli	rabbit	**sto foúrno**	baked
krasí	wine	**tiganitó**	fried
kréas	meat	**tyrí**	cheese
melitzánes	aubergines	**xifías**	swordfish

PLACES TO EAT

Price categories refer to meals per person with modest intake of wine, beer or raki. Except where indicated, reservations are rarely necessary (or even possible) – one waits, or an extra table may be fitted in.

€€€€ over 33 euros   €€ 15–24 euros
€€€ 24–33 euros   € under 15 euros

IRÁKLIO AND CENTRAL CRETE

Alekos €€€€ *Behind Agía Pelagía church, Vóri, tel: 28920 91094.* After visiting Phaistos and Agía Triáda, head for this secluded village taverna. The setting – a courtyard with tables and cushioned bench seating, an interior with a fireplace – is matched by the food: hearty portions of deftly executed recipes. A woodburning oven bakes goat or kid dishes (ordered in advance). daily lunch and dinner, all year. Cash only.

Giakoumis € *Fotíou Theodosáki 8, Iráklio, tel: 2810 280277.* Popular classic market taverna specialises in succulent lamb chops, crispy potatoes, seasonal salads and equally good rosé or white bulk wine. Mon–Sat lunch and dinner, all year. Cash only.

Ippokambos €€ *Sofoklí Venizélou 3, Iráklio, tel: 2810 280240.* Highly regarded *ouzerí* by the Venetian harbour. Excellent *mezédes* (including snails), reasonably priced seafood and winning service. It gets busy, so go early; no reservations. Apr–Nov Mon–Sat lunch and dinner. Cash only.

Karnagio €€€€ *Mínoös 3, corner shore road, Tálos district, Iráklio, tel: 2810 280090.* A local favourite, tops for seafood like grilled cuttlefish or octopus, and rich risotto. Both scaly fish and shellfish are affordable, the house wine is also excellent. Daily all year, lunch and dinner. Credit cards accepted.

Kirkor € *Lion (Morosíni) Fountain Square, Iráklio, no phone.* Armenian-run stall with outdoor tables opposite the fountain, serving succulent *bougátsa* (custard pastry), *tyrópittes* (cheese pies) and good coffees since 1922, daily from dawn until evening.

Paradosiako €€ *Vourváhon 9, Iráklio, tel: 2810 342927.* Secluded, no-nonsense taverna with courtyard seating and intriguing objet trouvé interior, reached by a pedestrian passage; grills, *mezédes* and a few dishes of the day are the stock in trade, Mon–Sat 2pm–midnight. Cash only.

Votomos €€ *Near Lake Vótomos, Záros, tel: 28940 31301.* Trout specialists, relying on their own fish farm, though there are also lamb and chicken dishes. The setting, in the Psilorítis foothills near Crete's main mineral-water bottlers, is idyllic. Apr–Oct daily for lunch and dinner, winter weekends only.

ÁGIOS NIKÓLAOS AND THE EAST

Angistri €€€€ *Angathiás village centre, near Palékastro, tel: 28430 61598.* Some of the cheapest, and freshest fish in the region, straight from Nikolas' boat. His son and daughter grill and serve respectively. A few cooked dishes as well, plus superb views from the terrace by day. Open all year.

Avli €€ *Príngipa Georgíou 12, Ágios Nikólaos, tel: 28410 82479.* All the usual *ouzerí* standards, as well as desserts like lemon mousse. Polite service and a vine-shaded courtyard (*avlí* in Greek). The big plus is wine from their own vineyard in the Sitía mountains. Daily Apr–Oct, lunch and dinner. Cash only.

Balcony €€€€ *Foundalídou 19, Sitía, tel: 28430 25084, www.balcony-restaurant.com.* Widely travelled owner-chef Tonya Karandinou's menu juxtaposes nouvelle Cretan fare (rabbit with walnuts and rosemary, snails in goat's cheese sauce) with creative salads, and Mexican or Asian dishes. A legacy of her time running restaurants in Laguna Beach and London. Pricey wine list. Dinner only Apr–Oct.

Chrisofyllis €€€€ *Aktí Papá Pangálou, Kitroplatía cove, Ágios Nikólaos, tel: 28410 22705.* Creative *ouzerí* with platters like *sfoungáta* (onion-sausage soufflé), eggplant with graviéra cheese and beetroot in yoghurt-walnut sauce. A minimalist interior sports old photos (some are for sale). Open all year, noon until late.

Dionyssos €€ *Magoúla hamlet, Lassíthi Plain, tel: 28440 31672.* The menu is short and sweet here: grills, a dish of the day and a few own-made starters, accompanied by good wine from their own vineyard. Sit at the back of the dining room for views over the plateau. May–Oct 11am–11pm. Cash only.

Haroupia €€€€ *Pláka, opposite Spinalónga, tel: 28410 42510.* Something of an oddity in a seafood-mad resort, this very competent, Greek-patronised *ouzerí* straddling the through road does simpler, sustaining fare – *apáki*, mushrooms, dolmádes and rakí. Cash only.

Káto Zákros Bay €€ *Waterfront, Káto Zákros, tel: 28430 26887.* Tellingly, this taverna at one of eastern Crete's remotest bays gets the most local clientele, for the sake of home-grown vegetables and poultry, fair prices and decent quality. Open all day, Apr–Oct. Cash only.

Kohylia €€ *East quay, Mókhlos, tel: 28430 94432.* A reliable choice amongst several establishments here, also the oldest (founded 1902). Expect fresh artichokes in spring, stews, and daily casseroles like stuffed vegetables or *moussakás*. Respectful, non-pushy service. Feb–Nov, lunch and dinner.

Levante €€€€ *Stratigoú Samaíl 38, Ierápetra, tel: 28420 80585.* The most reliable of the consecutive tavernas behind the seafront with castle views, established since the 1930s. Homestyle dishes like milk-based *xýgalo*, stuffed cabbage leaves, *papoutsáki* and *omathiés* – rice-and-offal sausage. Open all year.

Zygos €€ *Kaló Horió centre, near Istron, tel: 28410 61389.* Whole goats roasting on spits out front announce this traditional taverna, with the management sourcing ingredients from their own farm. It can get raucous during the season, but Dimítris is a great host. Daily, all year, noon–11pm.

RÉTHYMNO, HANIÁ, THE SOUTHWEST

Anchorage €€ *Main access road, Soúgia, tel: 28230 51487*.
Forego sea views in favour of a vine-shaded courtyard and decent renditions of *angináres me koukiá* (artichoke hearts with broad beans), wild *hórta*, stewed rabbit, and *tsigaristó*. Daily Easter–Oct, noon–11pm. Cash only.

Halkina €€€€ *Aktí Tombazi 29–30, old harbour, Haniá, tel: 28210 41570*. Tucked inconspicuously between the tourist traps of the two Venetian ports is this *rakádiko*, well attended for titbits like eggplant roulade, *marathópita* (fennel pie) and *apáki*. Oddly, their bulk wine is preferable to their *rakí*. Daily from 1pm until late. Cash only.

Ifigeneia €€ *Angouseli* ná, west outskirts, 10km from Spíli or Plakiás, tel: 28320 51362*. A shrine of traditional Cretan delicacies like *volví skordal` áta* (pickled wild hyacinth bulbs), *stamnagáthi*, *apáki* and boiled goat with *gamopílafo* (white sticky rice). Nightly all year; booking suggested.

Kalamoti €€ *Venizélou 142, Halépa district, Haniá, tel: 28210 59198*. A favourite seaside hangout of locals, thanks to sizeable casserole dishes (these can sell out at lunch), vegetarian platters and seafood. Try dolmádes, *myzíthra* cheese or grilled *soupiá* (cutttlefish), accompanied by the decent local *retsína* (pine-resin-flavoured wine). Open all year.

Kyma €€ *On the seafront, Soúgia, tel: 28230 51688*. Kyma's is usually packed, for good reason – big portions of good-value fare like own-made *taramosaláta* and *marathópita*, with friendly service. Sadly, the seafood is often frozen, but there's quaffable bulk wine. Daily late Apr–late, Oct noon–11pm.

Lygaria €€€€ *Shoreline, Lake Kourná, tel: 28250 61695*. At the far end of the 'strip' here, Lygaria eschews (for the most part) picture-menus, relying instead on its excellent *apáki*, *stífno* greens, stuffed squash blossoms and chunky house *melitsanosaláta* to draw customers. Open all year (weekends only winter).

Ouzythino €€ *Aktí Papanikolí, Neahóra district, Haniá, tel: 28210 73315.* Ask locals where they go for seaside dining when they tire of the Venetian harbours, and they'll direct you to Neahóra, just west of the old town. This is a popular taverna, thanks to the generous helpings of marinated anchovies, Sfakian sausages, courgette patties and cheese-stuffed peppers. Daily all year for lunch and dinner. Cash only.

Rakodikeio €€ *Vernádou 7, opposite Nerantzés Mosque, Réthymno, tel: 6945 774407.* This exquisite little *ouzerí*, a big hit with Réthymno's student contingent, offers creatively tweaked dishes like pork fried with saffron and ouzo. Mid-summer for dinner only, otherwise 2pm until very late. Cash only.

Strofi tis Yefsis € *Vyzári, Amári Valley, Akrotíri Peninsula, tel: 28330 41258 or 6944 470006.* An excellent lunch stop while touring the valley. Expect simple fare like rabbit, snails and chips cut as medallions, washed down by their own strong wine. Open all year, as and when. Cash only.

Tamam €€€€ *Zambeliou 49, Evraïkí district, Haniá, tel: 28210 96080.* This former *hamam* built in 1645 contains one of the best, most atmospheric restaurants in town. The fare is Cretan, plus Mediterranean/Middle Eastern specialities like Iranian pilaf and lots else for vegetarians. Daily all year for lunch and dinner.

The Third Eye €€ *Some 50m inland from west beach, south end, Paleohóra, tel: 28230 42223.* A remarkable vegetarian restaurant, with an extensive Asian/Indian menu plus a range of desserts. Breakfast also offered; occasional concerts by night. All day from before Easter to end Oct.

Zorbas € *Behind the giant eucalyptus, near bus stop, Stavrós, Akrotíri peninsula, tel: 28210 39402.* Generally we run a mile from tavernas so named, but this one's the real deal – the most locally attended of several on this sandy cove, where the disastrous log-transport scene of *Zorba the Greek* was filmed. There's a good range of seafood, cheeses, lamb dishes and vegetable casseroles in big portions. Open all year. Cash only.

A–Z TRAVEL TIPS

A Summary of Practical Information

A

ACCOMMODATION (See also Recommended Hotels, page 137)

Hotels: Many resort hotels have contracts with tour operators. If travelling between mid-July and early September, always make a firm reservation before arrival to avoid disappointment. April–May and October prices are generally much lower than at peak season. Most resort hotels close from November to March inclusive, although hotels in the largest north coast towns stay open all year.

Rooms, Apartments and Studios: Except at the top end of the quality scale, the vast majority of accommodation in Crete is in modern, purpose-built blocks of rooms, studios or apartments, usually family-owned and run, simply furnished, but almost always immaculately clean. The fancier places may be small complexes built around a pool and a small bar or restaurant. Apartments and studios will have some form of cooking facilities, and larger apartments may have up to three bedrooms, ideal for families.

In the UK, agencies specialising in packages for high-quality self-catering premises and hotels include Pure Crete (tel: 01444 881402, www.purecrete.com), Sunvil (tel: 020 8568 4499, www.sunvil.co.uk), The Villa Collection (tel: 020 8232 9780, www.gicthevilla collection.com) and Cachet Travel (tel: 020 8847 8700, www.cachet-travel.co.uk).

I'd like a single/double room with bath/shower	**Tha íthela éna monóklino/díklino me bánio/dous**
How much (does it cost)?	**Póso káni?**

AIRPORTS

International, charter and domestic flights to Crete serve the airports at **Iráklio** (HER), for central and eastern resorts, and **Haniá** (CHQ) for the western part of the island. The airport at **Sitía** (JSH), in the far east, only has domestic flights for now; an ambitious expansion of the terminal to accept international ones has stalled for lack of funds.

Iráklio is the biggest airport, and can get horribly crowded at times: there's a bus service the 5km (3 miles) to and from Platía Eleftherías in the centre of town until late at night. There is also bus service from Haniá airport the 14km (8½ miles) to the city, but so infrequently (6 daily) that most arrivals take taxis – the only option at Sitía, barring a 1,200-metre downhill walk into town.

B

BICYCLE AND SCOOTER HIRE *(Rental)*

Bicycle hire: The mountains make long-distance cycle touring on Crete very hard work, but in most resorts you can hire mountain bikes, and they'll usually offer good advice on where to explore. Some local travel agents also offer easy bike tours, with a bus to take you up the hills and carry your gear.

Scooter hire: Hiring a small motorbike is inexpensive – around €15 per day for a 50cc machine, less if you hire for three days or more. It is illegal to ride a bike with any size engine without a motorcycle licence – but many hire agencies ignore this legislation. If you ride a motorbike without the right licence, any insurance you have will be void and could create grave difficulties if you are involved in an accident; quad bikes, also widely available, are legal to drive with Class B car licenses. Blue Sea, Kosmá Zótou 5 (Ikostipémptis Avgoústou) is a reliable Iráklio company that hires scooters and motorbikes (tel: 28102 41097; www.blue searentals.com).

What's the hire charge for a full day?	**Póso kostízi giá mía méra?**

BUDGETING FOR YOUR TRIP

Crete offers good value for money, especially compared to most other parts of Greece. Here are some approximate prices to help you to plan your budget.

Flight from Athens to Iráklio	€35–100 by season
Adult ferry ticket from Athens	€35/60 (basic/in cabin)
High-season room in mid-range hotel	€75–100 per night
Meal in mid-range taverna per person	€15–20
Taxi fare from airport to Haniá	€24
Entrance fee for museums/sites	€2–6
Car hire (prebooked): small car for two weeks	€320

C

CAMPING

There are camp sites near most major towns and resorts: extremely busy in July and August, and aimed mainly at camper vans. Rough camping is officially prohibited, but communities of free campers form at 'alternative' havens like Soúgia, Léndas, Falássarna and on the offshore islet of Gávdos.

CAR HIRE *(Rental)*

The best car hire rates (under €25 per day) apply to periods of four days or more, with unlimited mileage. Distances on Crete can be considerable, so limited mileage tariffs are rarely cost effective. One-way rentals (pick up at one airport, drop off at another) incur surcharges of €35–70.

Reserving before you arrive through an international hire company can be useful, as in peak s eason demand will be high. Some of the best consolidator websites include www.skycars.co.uk, www.auto-europe.co.uk/com, www.carrentals.co.uk, and www. rentalcargroup.com. **Alianthos** (tel: 28320 31851; www.alianthos-group.com) is an excellent local operator, with offices at airports and major resorts.

You will need a credit card for a damages deposit and a full national licence (held for at least one year) from your country of residence. Non-EU license holders must by Greek law also have an International Driving Permit; failing this, many agencies will refuse to release the car, and if police detect you, fines are getting on for €1000. Depending on the model and the hire company, the minimum age for hiring a car varies from 21 to 25. Third-party liability insurance and Collision Damage Waiver is usually included in the stated rate, but there is usually a large excess (typically €400) before CDW takes effect. One reputable outfit selling such policies is Insurance4CarHire (www.insurance4carhire.com).

CLIMATE

Crete has an average of 320 sunny days per year. Winters are mild, although it can suddenly become cold and wet for short spells. In general, the south coast is hotter, drier and less windy than the north. About 70 percent of the annual rainfall falls between December and March. These are the approximate monthly average temperatures in Iráklio:

		J	F	M	A	M	J	J	A	S	O	N	D
Air (max)	°C	16	16	18	21	24	28	30	39	28	26	21	19
	°F	60	60	64	70	76	82	86	86	82	78	70	66
Air (min)	°C	9	9	10	12	16	18	20	22	20	17	14	11
	°F	48	48	50	54	60	64	68	72	68	62	57	52
Sea	°C	16	16	17	18	20	23	24	25	24	23	19	17
	°F	61	61	63	64	68	73	75	77	75	73	66	63

CLOTHING

Away from the beach, you should be fully clothed – Greeks take offence at bare or barely clad torsos of either sex. For sightseeing, bring shorts or lightweight trousers/dresses and T-shirts, along with comfortable shoes for visiting archaeological sites. When visiting churches or monasteries, men should wear trousers and women a skirt that covers the knees; both sexes should cover their shoulders. For evenings, few places have a dress code, though smarter hotel dining-rooms require men to wear long trousers in the evenings. If travelling in the mountains, sudden changes in weather require that you take an extra layer of clothing.

CRIME AND SAFETY *(See also Emergencies)*

Crete is a relatively safe island to visit, with little major crime. However, petty crime and burglaries are on the increase so take precautions: leave valuables in your room safe and don't carry large amounts of cash around. If you are a crime victim, you will need to contact the local ordinary police in the first instance; insurance claims will not be valid without their paperwork.

D

DRIVING

Road conditions: Crete's roads have improved such that few parts of the island are now inaccessible to a normal hire car. However, most roads have no paved shoulders, which can cause problems if you need to slow and leave the highway. Roads in the interior may be steep, with hairpin turns – always allow extra time even for apparently short distances. Fellow road users frequently include herds of goats and sheep. The north coast 'motorway' between Kíssamos and Sitía corresponds more to a UK 'A' road, with just a single lane in each direction (slow traffic straddles the white line to the right) and whole sections still unfinished between Mália and Sitía.

Rules and regulations: Greece drives on the right and (theoretically) passes on the left. Cretan drivers observe their own rules, often pulling over with no warning to talk to friends, or driving on the wrong side of the road. The largest towns have one-way systems to ease the flow of traffic around the narrow streets, but many motorcyclists (and some car drivers) do not obey these rules. Always expect the unexpected.

Speed limits: 100 kph (65 mph) on open roads and 50 kph (30 mph) in towns, although most local drivers do not adhere to these limits and tailgate 'slowcoaches' mercilessly. Both speed-limit and distance signs are in kilometres. Seat belts are compulsory, as are crash helmets when riding a motorbike – non-observance will net you a draconian fine. Drink-driving laws are strict and control points can test you and pull you off the road instantly.

Road signs: Signs often come late, hidden by vegetation or not at all, but where they do exist are mostly international and easily understood, with names in both Roman script and Greek lettering.

Detour	**ΠΑΡΑΚΑΨΗ/Parákapsi**
Parking	**ΠΑΡΚΙΓΚ/Párking**
Forbidden	**...ΑΠΑΓΟΡΕΥΕΤΑΙ/...apagorévete**
Be careful	**ΠΡΟΣΟΧΗ/Prosohí**
Stop	**ΣΤΑΜΑΤΑ/Stamáta**
For pedestrians	**ΓΙΑ ΠΕΖΟΥΣ/Gia pezoús**
Danger	**ΚΥΝΔΙΝΟΣ/Kýndinos**
No entry	**ΑΠΑΓΟΡΕΥΕΤΑΙ Η ΕΙΣΟΔΟΣ/ Apagorévete i ísodos**

Fuel: Fuel in Crete is some of the most expensive in Greece, currently around €1.80 per litre. Petrol stations are reasonably common, but don't let your tank get too low, especially in the south. Many stations close on Sunday, and most shut by 9pm.

Parking: Although local drivers seem to park where they choose, there are enforced rules. Street parking is permissible, unless stated, but finding a space in towns may be a problem.

If you need help: Your car hire office should provide contact numbers for breakdown services. If you are involved in an accident with another vehicle, it is illegal to leave the scene – wait for the ordinary police or traffic police (*trohéa*) to show up and take statements.

Fill the tank please, with (lead-free) petrol	**Parakaló, gemíste i dexamení (me amólyvdi)**
My car has broken down	**To avtokínito mou éhi halási**

E

ELECTRICITY

The current in Crete is 220v/50Hz. Plugs and outlets are of the European continental two-prong type. North American visitors should bring dual-voltage shavers and hair dryers, as well as plug adaptors.

EMBASSIES AND CONSULATES

Australian Embassy and Consulate Level 6, Thon Building, junction Kifisías & Alexándras, 115 21 Athens; tel: 210 87 04 000, www.greece.embassy.australia.gov.au/

British Vice Consulate Candia Tower, Thalíta 17, Iráklio; tel: 2810 224012.

British Embassy and Consulate Ploutárhou 1, 106 75 Athens: tel: 210 72 72 600, http://ukingreece.fco.gov.uk/en/

Canadian Embassy Gennadíou 4, 115 21 Athens; tel: 210 72 73 400.

Irish Embassy Vassíleos Konstandínou 7, 106 74 Athens; tel: 210 72 32 771.

South African Embassy and Consulate Kifisías 60, 151 25 Marousi, Athens; tel: 210 61 06 645.

US Embassy and Consulate Vassilísis Sofías 91, 101 60 Athens; tel: 210 72 12 951; http://athens.usembassy.gov/

EMERGENCIES

Important telephone numbers:
Police (Emergency)   100
Ambulance   166
Fire   199

G

GAY AND LESBIAN TRAVELLERS

Crete has no specific gay scene but Haniá has long hosted a small community, and attitudes in the resorts are generally relaxed. Be discreet in the conservative rural communities. Homosexual practice is legal in Greece for people aged over 17 years old.

GETTING THERE

By Air: Greek airlines Olympic (www.olympicair.com) or Aegean (www.aegeanair.com) operate daily scheduled flights to Iráklio from Athens, Thessaloniki, Rhodes, slightly fewer to Haniá, and almost daily from Rhodes to Sitiá. Sky Express (www.skyexpress.gr), offers flights on tiny aircraft from many Greek islands to Iráklio, as well as more unusual routes to Sitiá. Book well in advance in summer.

Direct scheduled flights from the UK are operated by EasyJet (www.easyjet.com), Thomas Cook (www.flythomascook.com) and Jet2 (www.jet2.com), but many visitors arrive on charter aircraft. A number of British tour operators offer flight-only and package deals from many UK airports; German, French, Italian and Swiss companies also fly in from around Europe.

By Boat: There are daily car and passenger ferries from Athens (Piraeus) to Iráklio and Haniá, plus two a week between Kíssamos and the Peloponnese, and about as frequently to Sitiá. Sailing time varies from 7 to 9 hours for the first three ports; Sitiá takes over 20 hours to reach. The major companies are Minoan Lines (tel: 2810 399800; www.minoan.gr) and ANEK (tel: 210 41 97 470;

www.anek.gr). General websites quoting up-to-date schedules include www.gtp.gr and www.openseas.gr.

GUIDES AND TOURS

You can hire a personal, officially licensed guide to accompany you around Knossos; you will find them at the site entrance beyond the ticket office. For guides to other areas, the local tourist office will be able to provide you with details. Many taxi drivers are also happy to act as unofficial guides to their local areas.

Tour companies in every resort offer a variety of day trips by coach or boat, as well as more adventurous jeep safaris in the mountains. Most obviously, you can visit the archaeological sites, Samariá Gorge, distant beaches and major towns of Crete from wherever you are staying on the island, simply look out for the advertising boards.

H

HEALTH AND MEDICAL CARE

There are no vaccination requirements for your trip to Crete. Emergency treatment is given free, although this only covers immediate needs. EU residents can get further free treatment with a European Health Insurance Card (EHIC; tel: 0845 6062030 in the UK; www.ehic.org.uk). It is advisable to take out additional travel insurance to cover you for protracted treatment or repatriation.

If you are taking any medication, bring enough for your holiday needs and keep it in its original packaging. If you have a basic medical need, look for a chemist, or *farmakío*, signified by a green cross, where you will be able to obtain advice. Most pharmacists speak some English.

Spiny sea urchins can cause serious injury if you step on or graze against them. Avoidance is the best option – they frequent rocky coasts with clean water. A more common nuisance is the mosquito, so always use insect repellent in the evenings. Tap water is safe to drink, and indeed excellent in the Cretan mountains.

Dial 166 for 24-hour ambulance dispatch. Each major town in Crete has its own hospital with an emergency ward (*epígonda peristatiká*):

Iráklio: 5km (3 miles) south of Iráklio; tel. 2810 237502.

Ágios Nikólaos: on Knossoú opposite the Archaeological Museum; tel: 28410 25221.

Réthymno: on Triandalídou 17; tel: 28310 27814.

Haniá: in Mourniés district; tel: 28210 22000.

a doctor/dentist	**énas giatrós/odontogiatrós**
hospital	**nosokomío**
an upset stomach	**anakatoméno stomáhi**

L

LANGUAGE

The sounds of the Greek language do not always correspond to exact equivalents in English, and the letters of the Greek alphabet do not always have a match in the Roman alphabet. This accounts for the divergent spellings of the same place name on Cretan road signs – for example, the word *ágios* is often also spelled *ághios* and *áyios* in the Roman alphabet, although it is always pronounced the same. Emphasis is also a vital element in pronouncing Greek. Throughout this book we have accented vowels within each Greek word to show which syllable to stress.

Most people working within the tourist industry will have a basic English vocabulary and many speak English very well. The *Berlitz Greek Phrase Book and Dictionary* covers nearly all the situations you're likely to encounter on your travels.

The table *(see opposite)* lists the Greek letters in their upper- and lower-case forms, followed by the Roman letters used in this book to transcribe them, and a pronunciation guide.

Α	α	a	as in f**a**ther
Β	β	v	as in **v**eto
Γ	γ	g	as in **g**o (except before *i* and e sounds, when it's like the y in **y**es)
Δ	δ	d	sounds like th in **th**en
Ε	ε	e	as in g**e**t
Ζ	ζ	z	same as in English
Η	η	i	as in sk**i**
Θ	θ	th	as in **th**in
Ι	ι	i	as in sk**i**
Κ	κ	k	same as in English
Λ	λ	l	same as in English
Μ	μ	m	same as in English
Ν	ν	n	same as in English
Ξ	ξ	x	as in bo**x**
Ο	ο	o	as in r**o**ad
Π	π	p	same as in English
Ρ	ρ	r	same as in English
Σ	σ, ς	s	as in ki**ss**, except like z before *m* or *g* sounds
Τ	τ	t	same as in English
Υ	υ	y	as in co**u**ntry
Φ	φ	f	same as in English
Χ	χ	h	rough, as in Scottish lo**ch**
Ψ	ψ	ps	as in ti**ps**y
Ω	ω	o	as in r**o**ad
ΑΙ	αι	e	as in h**ay**
ΑΥ	αυ	av	as in **av**ant-garde
ΕΙ	ει	i	as in sk**i**
ΕΥ	ευ	ev	as in **ev**er
ΟΙ	οι	i	as in sk**i**
ΟΥ	ου	ou	as in rec**ou**p
ΓΓ	γγ	ng	as in lo**ng**er
ΓΚ	γκ	g	as in **g**one
ΓΞ	γξ	nx	as in a**nx**ious
ΜΠ	μπ	b	as in **b**eg or com**p**ass
ΝΤ	ντ	d or nd	as in **d**og or u**nd**er

M

MAPS

Most maps of Crete are surprisingly inaccurate, with all showing the minor roads differently. Free maps from car hire companies are often no worse than commercial ones. Top touring coverage is provided by publisher Anavasi; they also do the best topographical maps for hiking.

MEDIA

Newspapers: Major English newspapers can be bought in resorts one day after publication. Some English tabloids have European editions printed in Greece and available the same day. The daily *Ekathimerini* (www.ekathimerini.com) included inside the *International Herald Tribune* is also available, as is the English-language *Athens News (www.athensnews.gr)*, published each Friday.

Television and Radio: Most large hotels have satellite TV services, which include news channels such as CNN and BBC World.

MONEY

Currency: For the time being, the euro (€) is used in Greece. Notes are denominated in 5, 10, 20, 50, 100, 200 and 500 euros; coins in 1 and 2 euros and 1, 2, 5, 10, 20 and 50 cents, known as *leptá* in Greece. Notes of 100 euros and above are regarded with suspicion, as counterfeit, and can often only be broken down in banks.

Currency exchange: Most banks exchange foreign currency but charge a commission (usually 1–3 percent) for the service. Exchange rates appear on a digital display, and are generally the same for each bank. You can also change money at bureaux de change, found in many tourist centres and open longer hours than banks. Some advertise commission-free transactions, but exchange rates are often inferior to those of banks.

Cash machines (ATMs): There are ATMs in every Cretan town or resort of over a few hundred inhabitants. These are the most convenient way to get euros.

Credit cards: Many hotels, restaurants, travel agencies and shops accept credit cards, but there is still a sizeable minority that do not, and out in the countryside credit cards are not generally accepted.

Travellers cheques: These are not recommended for use in Greece – expect severe delays or outright refusals in banks or bureaux.

OPENING TIMES

Opening times vary between official organisations and privately owned shops and cafés, and also between high and low season. Almost everybody closes at mid-afternoon, and official entities will not reopen later; if you need to get anything official done, do so in the morning.

Banks are open Mon–Thur 8am–2.30pm, Fri 8am–2pm. Monday is a typical day of closure for museums, though major attractions will open daily (if perhaps only Monday afternoon).

Shops are open Monday, Wednesday and Saturday 9am–2.30pm, closing at 2pm on Tuesday, Thursday and Friday but open additionally 5.30–8.30pm. Supermarkets open 9am–9pm Mon–Fri, 9am–8pm Sat; a very few may work 10am–4pm Sunday.

POLICE

Regular police officers wear two-toned blue uniforms. Tourist police (found in Iráklio, Haniá, Ágios Nikólaos and Hersónisos) also wear blue uniforms displaying a small national flag indicating which language they speak other than Greek. Main police stations are located as follows:

Iráklio: Dikeosínis 10; tel: 2810 283190.

Ágios Nikólaos: Erythroú Stavroú 47; tel: 28410 26900.
Réthymno: Eleftheríou Venizélou 20; tel: 28310 28156.
Haniá: Iraklíou 23; tel: 28210 73333.

POST OFFICES

Post offices (7.30am–2pm) have blue-and-yellow livery, and are marked 'Elliniká Takhydromía' in Greek plus 'Hellenic Post' in English. Stamps can be bought here, or at postal agencies (usually small shops) for a small premium. Packages for non-EU countries should not be sealed until they have been checked by post office staff.

Mail boxes are yellow, but in rural areas they are not emptied every day. Most hotels will post letters and postcards for you. Allow 4–7 days for postcards to Europe, 9–14 days for the rest of the world.

| A stamp for this letter/ postcard | **Éna grammatósimo gi'aftó to grámma/gi'aftí tin kart postál** |

PUBLIC HOLIDAYS

National holidays fall on the following dates:

1 January	New Year's Day *(Protohroniá)*
6 January	Epiphany *(Theofánia)*
25 March	Greek Independence/Annunciation *(Evangelismós)* Day
1 May	May Day
15 August	Dormition *(Kímisis)* of the Virgin
28 October	National *Óhi* ('No') Day
25 December	Christmas *(Hristoúgena)*
26 December	Gathering of the Virgin's Entourage *(Sýnaxis tis Panagías)*

Moveable dates: The first day of Lent (Clean Monday/*Katharí Deftéra*), Good Friday, Easter Monday and Whit Monday/*Agíou Pnévmatos*.

R

RELIGION

The population is almost 100 percent Greek Orthodox. However, Roman Catholic churches hold regular masses at Iráklio, Ágios Nikólaos, Haniá and Réthymno. There is a sizable Armenian community with its own church in Iráklio, and the Haniá synagogue conducts Friday evening services.

T

TELEPHONES

Since deregulation of the local telecoms market, a number of providers offer competition to the state-run OTE. OTE still, however, maintains most of the increasingly scarce public booths. Kiosks and newsagents sell OTE calling-cards in various unit denomination, as well as other products (including discount long-distance cards and local mobile top-up cards).

Most hotels of two-star rating and above have direct-dial lines, but add a huge surcharge to the cost of calls. Avoid this by using a prepaid, 12-digit-code card with an access number.

The international code for Greece is 30. Within Greece, all phone numbers have ten digits; fixed lines begin with 2, mobiles with 6.

Foreign visitors with tri-band mobiles can roam on one of the four Greek networks, but charges (despite intra-EU capping) remain extortionate. If you are staying more than a week or two, it makes sense to buy a local SIM with some talk-time included. It must be registered at time of purchase, but the number remains valid for a year from each top-up.

TIME ZONES

Greece is two hours ahead of Greenwich Mean Time and also observes Daylight Savings along with the rest of Europe (but not the

USA), moving clocks one hour forward between the last Sunday in March and the last one in October.

In August, here is the time in the following cities:

New York	London	Dublin	Jo'burg	**Crete**	Sydney	Auckland
5am	10am	10am	11am	**noon**	7pm	9pm

TIPPING

Service is notionally included in restaurant bills, although it is customary to leave between 5 and 10 percent of the bill in small change on the table. Hotel chambermaids should be left a tip of around €1 per day.

TOILETS

Large towns will have public toilets, usually near the marketplace or bus station. If attended, there is usually a €0.50 fee to the warden. Most museums have good public facilities.

Older sewage pipes in Greece are narrower than in most European countries and are easily clogged. Never put toilet paper into the toilet – always use the waste bin provided.

TOURIST INFORMATION

The Greek National Tourist Organisation, or Ellinikós Organismós Tourismoú (EOT; www.visitgreece.gr), is responsible for producing and dispersing tourist information. For information before you travel to Greece, contact one of the following offices.

Australia: 37–49 Pitt Street, Sydney, NSW; postal address: PO Box R203 Royal Exchange, NSW 2000; tel: (2) 9241 1663.

UK and Ireland: 4 Conduit Street, London W1R 0DJ; tel: (020) 7495 9300.

US: 305 East 47th Street, New York, NY 10017; tel: (212) 421 5777.

For local tourist information, contact one of the following addresses:

Ágios Nikólaos: Aktí Koundoúrou; tel: 28410 22357.

Haniá: Kydonías 29, inside the city hall; tel: 28210 36155; www.chania.gr.

Iráklio: Zanthoudídou 1, opposite the Archaeological Museum; tel: 28102 46298; www.heraklion.gr.

Réthymno: Delfini Building, Sofoklí Venizélou, town beach; tel: 28310 29148; www.rethymnon.com.

TRANSPORT

Buses: An excellent network of affordable bus services crosses the island, with stops at all the major archaeological sites. Always arrive slightly ahead of departure time. Tickets are bought on the bus or in advance. Iráklio has two bus stations: on the main road by the ferry port for north-coast services, outside the Haniá Gate for towards Phaistos, Mátala and Agía Galíni. Réthymno bus station is west of the town centre just off the coast road; Haniá's is centrally located on Kydonías, and in Ágios Nikólaos some way out near the Archeological Museum. For timetables and useful information visit www.bus-service-crete-ktel.com.

Taxis: Taxis are numerous, and fares are regulated, but with surcharges for baggage and serving airports. They should have working meters that are set upon departure (to €1.20, not zero; minimum fare €3.20). Agree on an hourly or daily rate before you set off.

Boats: Many resort ports are home to seasonal excursion boats, while various south-coast settlements are better connected by scheduled ferry services than by road. The main towns for taking boat trips are Ágios Nikólaos, Agía Galíni and Haniá, while daily ferries ply between Hóra Sfakíon, Loutró, Soúgia and Paleóhora.

What's the fare to… ?	**Póso éhi éna isitírio giá…?**
When's the next bus to… ?	**Póte févgi to epómeno leofório giá…?**

V

VISAS AND ENTRY REQUIREMENTS

European Union (EU) citizens may enter Greece for an unlimited length of time. British citizens must have a valid passport. Citizens of Ireland can enter with a valid identity card or passport. Citizens of the US, Canada, Australia and New Zealand can stay for up to 90 days within any 180-day period upon production of a valid passport; no advance visas are needed. South African citizens require a Schengen Visa, applied for in advance at a Greek embassy or consulate.

There are no limits on the amount of hard currency visitors can import or export, though amounts in excess of €10,000 equivalent should be declared.

W

WEBSITES

www.explorecrete.com useful general site with all sorts of info and links

www.greecetravel.com/crete the Crete page of Matt Barrett's acclaimed general Greek website

www.climbincrete.com one-stop resource for trekkers and rock-climbers

www.west-crete.com labour of love, with plenty of useful links, on all things found west of Réthymno

Y

YOUTH HOSTELS

There are just three youth hostels in Crete: in Plakiás, Réthymno and Iráklio. None are members of the official youth hostel movement. You can book them at websites such as www.hostels.com; the Plakiás one has its own site, www.yhplakias.com.

Recommended Hotels

Hotels in Greece are officially rated by EOT according to the facilities available. The former system of De Luxe, A, B, C, D and E class is gradually being replaced by a 5-to-no-star categorisation.

Accommodation in private rooms or apartments is graded from one to three 'keys'. In every room you'll find an official price placard on the back of the door. You should never pay more than this, and, except at the busiest seasons – Easter week and August – the price ought to be significantly less.

Hotel booking websites can yield significant discounts at any time. Establishments below are open all year unless otherwise stated.

To dial the telephone numbers below from outside Greece you'll need to add the international country code +30. Prices are for a double room per night in high season.

€€€€€	over 170 euros
€€€€	120–170 euros
€€€	80–120 euros
€€	50–80 euros
€	50 euros and under

IRÁKLIO AND CENTRAL CRETE

Eva Marina € *Mátala resort, tel 28290 45125, www.evamarina. com.* Small, 1980s vintage hotel, with pine furniture and white tiles underfoot, set in lush gardens, a short distance from the sea. Open late Mar–Oct. 20 rooms.

Galaxy Hotel €€€€ *Dimokratías 75, 71 306 Iráklio, tel: 2810 238812, www.galaxy-hotel.com.gr.* The city's finest hotel, with recently refurbished rooms and suites (all the expected comforts), grand public spaces and willing service. Interior-facing rooms are quieter, and you lose nothing as regards the view. Facilities include a large pool, gym and *hammam* (steam room), restaurant and two bars (one at poolside). 127 rooms.

Lato €€€ *Epimenídou 15, 712 02 Iráklio, tel: 2810 228103, www.lato.gr.* Iráklio's first self-styled boutique hotel, with the best, balconied rooms or suites facing the Venetian harbour (singles are very small). Walkable to all attractions yet reasonably quiet at night.

Marin Dream €€€ *Doukós Bofór 12, 712 02 Iráklio, tel: 2810 300018, www.marinhotel.gr.* Another boutique hotel with sweeping port views from the spacious front rooms – again, singles are tiny. A good breakfast is provided at the roof restaurant (not otherwise recommended). 43 rooms.

Villa Kynthia €€€€–€€€€€ *Pánormos resort, tel: 28340 51102, winter 2810 228723, www.villakynthia.gr.* A beautifully renovated, personally managed 1890s mansion-inn in this coastal village between Iráklio and Réthymno. Each of five units (2 rooms, 2 suites, 1 apartment) is individually furnished with antiques; common areas comprise a courtyard with small pool, breakfast lounge and bar. Open Mar–Nov; winter by arrangment.

ÁGIOS NIKÓLAOS AND THE EAST

Big Blue €–€€ *west edge of town, by Roman cistern, 720 56 Mýrtos, tel: 28420 51094, www.big-blue.gr.* Choose from three grades of lodging at this ecologically-run complex with the best views in this resort. Breakfast served in terrace garden; extremely knowledgable proprietor. 4 rooms, 6 studios and 2 apartments.

Du Lac €€ *Ikostiogdóis Oktovríou 17, 721 00 Ágios Nikólaos, tel: 28410 22711, www.dulachotel.gr.* Right beside Lake Voulisméni in the heart of the action, the excellent-value Du Lac offers a mix of designer-decor rooms and studios (the latter effectively 1-bed apartments), half of which overlook the water. Convenient ground-floor restaurant and café. 24 rooms.

El Greco € *Arkadíou 13, 723 00 Sitía, tel: 28430 23133, www.elgreco-sitia.gr.* Best-value and friendliest hotel in the town centre, with 2007-redone rooms, good views from the higher ones and a pleasant lobby. Only down side: tricky street parking.

Elounda Mare €€€€€ *720 53 Eloúnda, tel: 28410 68200, www. eloundamare.com.* Stablemate of the co-managed Porto Elounda complex (many facilities are shared), the Elounda Mare strikes a warmer, more intimate note, especially in bungalows and bunga-low-suites with fireplaces, wood floors and private sea-water pools. The multi-levelled lounge and common areas continue outside as lovely terraced grounds lead down to stone lidos – there's little real beach here. Open late Apr–late Oct.

Istron Bay €€€€–€€€€€ *Istron, 721 00 Ágios Nikólaos, tel: 28410 61303, www.istronbay.gr.* Some 13km (8 miles) southeast of Ágios Nikólaos, this old-fashioned hillside complex remains competitive by dominating one of the area's best beaches. Among four grades of accommodation, choose superior standard or above. Open Apr–Oct.

Kakkos Bay €€ *Koutsounári, 9km east of Ierápetra, tel: 28420 61241, www.kakkosbay.com.* 1980s-vintage but very pleasant re-sort scattered amidst well-tended gardens, pines and olive trees. Spacious bungalows (preferable to standard rooms) resembling Cre-tan country chapels from outside. A pool with all-day restaurant seems superfluous, since the complex brackets one of the calmest sandy coves in the region, sheltered from prevailing winds. Open May–Oct. 33 standard rooms, 27 bungalows.

Knossos Royal Village €€€€–€€€€€ *700 14 Liménas Hersoníssou, tel: 28970 27400, www.aldemarhotels.com.* This self-contained re-sort features low-rise units in three grades scattered across a large verdant plot. Family-friendly amenities include pools, restaurants, bars, shops, kids' club, tennis courts and watersports. Guests can book treatments at the adjacent Aldemar Thalasso Spa. 364 units.

Marina Village €€ *behind Kouremérnos beach, 723 00 Palékastro, tel: 28430 61284, www.palaikastro.com/marinavillage.* The three small wings of this 1980s hotel are idyllically set in olive groves and orchards, if a bit hard to find (follow the signs). Common areas in-clude a pool, tennis court and shady breakfast gazebo. Open 15 Apr–31 Oct.

St Nicolas Bay Resort Hotel and Villas €€€€€ *PO Box 47, 721 00 Ágios Nikólaos, tel: 28410 25041, www.stnicolasbay.gr.* On the Nisí peninsula overlooking Mirabéllo Bay 1.5km (1 mile) north of town, the stone-clad St Nicolas Bay Resort offers discreet luxury with a degree of privacy for its suite-sized standard rooms, superior suites with private infinity pools, and a cluster of 3-or-4-bedroom villas with a private lido. Sandy coastline is limited to one small cove, but there's a full watersports programme and 34-foot sailing boat to charter. A spa, kid's club and several (pricey) à la carte restaurants complete the picture. 107 units. Open Apr–Oct.

Stella's Traditional Apartments €€–€€€ *Káto Zákros, 72300 Sitía, tel: 28430 23739, www.stelapts.com.* Looking down over the local oasis to the eastern edge of Crete, these comfortable apartments are set in lush terrace-gardens with hammocks. There's spring water on tap and a sense of complete peace.

RÉTHYMNO, HANIÁ AND THE WEST

Anna's House €€€–€€€€ *300m across river bridge, en route Vámos, Georgioúpoli, tel: 28250 61556, www.annashouse.gr.* More accurately Anna's houses, comprising four grades of rooms, spacious apartments and villas, in landscaped grounds around a large pool. Open 15 Mar–15 Nov.

Casa Delfino €€€€€ *Theofánous 9, Tophanás, 731 00 Haniá, tel: 28210 93098, www.casadelfino.com.* High-quality hotel where designer fittings are juxtaposed with recycled timber. The premises have been renovated by a descendent of the 19th century Genoese Delfino family which originally built this mansion. Differing units all have handmade Italian furniture and marble or solid wood flooring. New since 2011 are 3 suites in an adjacent building, a spa and roof-terrrace bar. 20 suites, 4 standard rooms.

Doma €€–€€€ *Venizélou 124, Halépa, 731 33 Haniá, tel: 28210 51772, www.hotel-doma.gr.* This converted neo-Classical mansion was once the Austro-Hungarian, then British Consulate. Now it's one of the gems of Crete, neither stuffy or luxurious but appealing to those who want a low-key yet personal stay recalling the genteel old days. The dining room serves Cretan specialities for breakfast and pre-booked dinner. Open Apr–Oct. 25 units.

Fortezza €€€ *Melissinoú 16, 741 00 Réthymno, tel: 28310 55551, www.fortezza.gr*. This modern yet stylish hotel on the north side of the old quarter, just below the Venetian fortress, is handy for the town centre and waterfront, yet quiet. Comfortable, air-conditioned rooms, renovated in 2011, represent great value; medium-sized pool in the courtyard. 50 rooms, 3 suites.

Heracles € *Below through road, 740 53 Spíli, tel: 28320 22111, e-mail: heraclespapadakis@hotmail.com*. The quietest and best-run of three extant lodgings in this mountain town, Heracles has well-kept balconied rooms with bug-screens; the owner is a mine of information about the area. Breakfast included in rates; bicycles rented. 5 rooms.

Milia Mountain Retreat €€–€€€ *730 12 Vlátos, tel: 28210 46774, www.milia.gr*. This 'eco-lodge' is nestled in the hills of western Crete, off a secondary road between Kíssamos and Paleóhora. Old stone cottages of different sizes (2–4 persons) have open fireplaces for cool nights. An excellent affiliated taverna serves up three meals daily, based on local produce. By day you can hike through nearby gorges or take painting courses; nights are spent gazing at the stars. 13 units.

Porto Loutro €€ *Loutró, tel: 28250 91433, www.hotelporto loutro.com*. Vehicle-free Loutró is accessible only by boat or on foot, so is wonderfully peaceful at night. This is the best hotel here, though still zen-minimalist. Two white-painted wings shelter standard rooms and studios with beamed ceilings and slate or marble flooring. The big attraction is taking in the sea view and slowing down to local pace from your balcony. Open mid-Mar–end Oct. Cash only.

Porto del Colombo €€€€€ *Theofánous 7, Tophanás, 731 10 Haniá, tel: 28210 70945, www.portodelcolombo.gr*. This historic

Venetian mansion is now a luxurious inn, completely refurbished during 2010 in mock-medieval style. Rooms, especially the galleried maisonettes, are large, with carved-wood furniture and coloured tiles plus proper shower stalls in the bathrooms. There are also 2-bedroom apartments adjacent. 10 rooms, 3 apartments.

Theresa €–€€ *Angélou 8, Tophanás, 731 00 Haniá, tel: 28210 92798, www.pensiontheresa.gr.* This characterful, budget pension occupies has en suite, often galleried rooms, accessed by a serpentine wooden staircase; the best are on the first floor. If you arrive and reception is unattended, simply book yourself in. There's a small kitchen, and roof terrace for great views over the harbour. Breakfast is available next door at Café Meltemi where the owner, Giorgos Nikitas, often sits. 7 rooms.

Vámos €€€€€ *730 08 Vámos (midway between Réthymno and Haniá), tel: 28250 22190, www.vamosvillage.gr.* Restored, stone-built houses scattered through Vámos old town, just 20 minutes from the sea. Most are maisonettes, with bedroom and bath upstairs, fireplace-lounges downstairs. Accommodation ranges from 2-person apartments to houses suitable for up to 8, with private or shared pool. There's an affiliated taverna, self-guiding walks and cooking courses held in an abandoned olive mill. 20 units.

Veneto €€€€ *Epimenídou 4, 741 00 Réthymno, tel: 28310 56634, www.veneto.gr.* One of the better inns occupying 14th-century Venetian buildings in the old quarter, with an acclaimed in-house restaurant (half-board rates given). Public areas – including a large, arcaded courtyard with three potable springs, where breakfast is served – somewhat overshadow the rooms; upper-storey ones are airier and balconied. 6 studios, 4 suites.

Zafiri 2 €€ *100m back from Pahiá Ammos (west) beach, 730 01 Paleóhora, tel: 28230 41811, www.zafiri-studios.com.* Studios and apartments on a quiet lane, with spacious, pleasant bedsit areas and long, narrow balconies affording limited sea views, though bathrooms are dated. The USP is the vast front lawn-garden where guests take their breakfast. 7 studios, 4 apartments.

INDEX

Berlitz® **pocket guide**

Crete

Eleventh Edition 2012
Reprinted 2013

Written by Lindsay Bennett
Updated by Marc Dubin
Edited by Paula Soper
Series Editor: Tom Stainer

Photography credits
APA/Pete Bennett 111; Berlitz 43; Donna Dailey
53; Fotolia.com/Paul Cowan 66;
Fotolia.com/Brad Pict 65; Fotolia.com/Panos 74;
Fotolia.com/Tim 70; APA/Glyn Genin 1, 12, 13,
17, 18, 19, 20, 22, 27, 38, 47, 49, 50, 57, 59, 63, 69,
82, 85, 92, 102, 105; GNTO 3BR, 3TL, 4BL, 5BR,
5TL, 8, 15, 72, 77, 80, 99; iStockphoto 4-5, 25, 30,
54, 61, 78, 95, 101; APA/Britta Jaschinski 2TL,
3CR, 4TL, 5TR, 10, 11, 33, 35, 37, 41, 45, 48, 86,
88, 90, 97, 106, 108; Topham Picturepoint 26, 28;
APA/Gregory Wrona 56, 64.

Cover picture: 4Corners Images

Contact us

At Berlitz we strive to keep our guides as
accurate and up to date as possible, but if you
find anything that has changed, or if you have
any suggestions on ways to improve this guide,
then we would be delighted to hear from you.

Berlitz Publishing, PO Box 7910,
London SE1 1WE, England.
email: berlitz@apaguide.co.uk
www.insightguides.com/berlitz